MW01194061

SENIORS ARE PEOPLE, TOO!

Exceptional Ministry with Seniors
in a Youth-focused Culture

by
J. D. MOSELEY

Sage Ministries Publications
Nashville, Tennessee

SENIORS ARE PEOPLE, TOO!
Exceptional Ministry with Seniors
in a Youth-focused Culture

www.sageministries.us

copyright © 2008 by J. D. Moseley
All rights reserved
This book or parts thereof may not be reproduced in any form, stored in a retrieval system, or transmitted in any form by any means – electronic, mechanical, photocopy, recording, by any information storage, or otherwise – without prior written permission of the Publisher, except as provided by United States of America copyright law.

Sage Ministries Publications, 5408 San Marcos Drive, Nashville, TN 37220

International Standard Book Number 978-0-9818523-0-0

Printed in the United States of America

First Printing, June 2008

Cover design by Luther Weathers

CONTENTS

ACKNOWLEDGMENTS

The Apostle Paul likened the church to a body where the different parts, regardless of appearance, each have value and all work together for a common purpose. I have seen that analogy beautifully lived out in the process of writing this book. Several have played invaluable roles in proof-reading and editing my initial efforts. Their input has literally saved me from myself.

My heartfelt thanks go out to Ms Giddy and Ms Joys. I trusted them first to see this effort in its most discordant state. Kudos also go out to Robbie whose eagle eyes helped shore up those annoying typos that defy cursory reviews and even "spell check." My hat is likewise off to Mat whose input is best described as "profound subtleties." I also owe a special thanks to Lauren and Helen whose "red ink" tightened up the text immeasurably by patiently and tirelessly pointing out areas of redundancies, overkill, and awkward wording.

This book truly is a cooperative effort that could not have been completed without the help of those who were willing to generously give their time and their hearts to the project. Praise God for how the body of Christ can work together as one to His glory.

In His Grace,
J. D. Moseley

PREFACE

There is something very exciting about providing a resource for others that attempts to offer enlightenment, inspiration, encouragement, motivation, and a fresh perspective on how to go about honoring God highly by serving others exceptionally. The prospect of providing such a resource is a daunting and arduous task but one that is especially satisfying when the need is so great and the cause happens to be one of God's all-time highest priorities. Although the words contained in this book have long ago become my own, I could not claim every thought or idea as original. At best, we are all only the product of what we have learned and personally experienced while rubbing shoulders with others along the journey of life with God. My objective is not to stake a claim on originality but rather to get the message out about the need for, as well as the value, importance, and urgency of *exceptional* ministry with today's seniors.

Throughout this book, there will be continual references to seniors ministry in comparison to youth ministry which could be perceived as "off topic" or perhaps even depreciating. These comparisons express neither the desire nor intent to diminish or denigrate the need for or the value, importance, and urgency of ministry with today's youth. To the contrary, I'm a big fan of youth ministry. In fact, I'm a double beneficiary. I was when I was an older teenage, and am now as a parent of three children and grandparent of one. We have all been richly blessed by exceptional youth ministry programs – for which I am forever grateful and eternally indebted. Rather, the continual comparative references to youth ministry are merely to help open the eyes and ears of hearts by placing seniors ministry in a different light and providing a "fresh eyes" perspective.

The many comparative references are intended to simply help us see ministry with today's seniors in a way that seniors ministry might otherwise never be seen – and to begin caring in a way we might not otherwise care. If the numerous comparative references to youth ministry become tiresome or perhaps even offensive, try seeing these comparisons as complimentary, rather than as uncomplimentary. So many churches are doing such an outstanding job with youth ministry that ministry with youth serves as an excellent standard by which churches and church leaders could measure many, if not all, of their other ministry efforts – including their ministry efforts with seniors.

By the grace of God, my objective is to simply make the message of this book as inspiring as it is informative and enlightening. My intent is to cast a vision before churches, church leaders, and other believers that will help them see the need for, as well as the value, importance, and urgency of ministry outreach to today's seasoned believers ... a vision that will help them live *exceptionally*.

- J. D. Moseley

CHAPTER ONE
Is There An Ophthalmologist In The House?
(seeing the need, value, importance, and urgency)

Open The Eyes Of My Heart

The message of a marvelous contemporary Christian song prayerfully pleads, *"Open the eyes of my heart. Open the eyes of my heart, Lord. I want to see You."* Such sentiments are as much a confession as they are a request acknowledging that sometimes we become blind to the reality that God has clearly laid before us. Who can forget the story of the prophet Elijah and his "blind" servant (2 Kings 6)? When faced with seemingly insurmountable odds, Elijah's assistant was blind to God's reality until Elijah prayed, "O *Lord, open his eyes so he may see.*" Until the Lord opened his eyes to the reality of legions of angelic warriors ready to assist in the challenges confronting them, he could not "see" God's reality in otherwise *seemingly* overwhelming circumstances.

Jesus spoke of times when some *"have eyes but fail to see, and ears but fail to hear"* (Mk. 8:18). In fact, when two disciples were on their way to Emmaus after the crucifixion, they didn't even recognize Jesus when He was standing among them until *"their eyes were opened"* (Lk. 24:31). Such blindness on our part to God's perspective occurs for various reasons - discouragement, fear, stubbornness, preconceptions, traditions, old paradigm thinking, worldly wisdom, pride, and, of course, trusting self more than God. One such perspective God has explicitly shared with His people is His priority for seniors.

Not A Nice Thing To Do

We can become involved in many good and worthwhile causes in the world. They may be humanitarian, philanthropical, political, environmental, social, cultural, etc. in nature. Involvement in or commitment to any of them is neither required nor necessary. They are just nice things to do, if we are so compelled or inclined.

For example, it's a nice thing to give to the Salvation Army or buy Girl Scout cookies. It's a nice thing to be part of an adopt-a-highway program to help keep our roadways beautiful or write a children's book that both entertains and educates. It's a

7

nice thing to recycle aluminum cans and cardboard boxes. It's a nice thing to rescue a pet from an animal shelter or buy high efficiency rated appliances that consume less energy. It's a nice thing to stay in shape.

Seniors ministry, however, is NOT a "nice thing to do." Although some things in life are simply "nice" things to do, ministry with seniors is not one of them. Given the relatively small amount of time, attention, and resources typically devoted to seniors ministry, you'd think it was merely a "nice" thing to do. Years ago Ted Koppel astutely quipped to our morally declining culture that the Ten Commandments were not the "Ten Suggestions." Seniors ministry is neither God's suggestion nor merely a nice thing to do if and only if we are so compelled or inclined. Rather, it has been clearly identified by God as one of His highest priorities since at least the days of Moses (as implied by the Fifth Commandment). This priority was repeated in the New Testament, not only by Jesus, but by Paul and James. James even identified placing a special focus on seniors as the very essence and epitome of authentic spirituality (James 1:27). When it comes to church budgets, ministry planning, and congregational priorities, seniors ministry is not just some discretionary nice thing to do, with an "*if-and-whether-we-get-around-to-it*" attitude.

The danger of seeing seniors ministry as merely "*a nice thing to do*" is that it blatantly exhibits absolute disregard for God's priority, not so unlike the practice of "corban" that supplanted God's priorities in the guise of being excusable (Mk. 7). Relegating seniors ministry to little more than a "leftovers" status may align with a youth-focused culture's priorities, but it's simply and sadly out of step with God's priorities. If we are to glean the full meaning of the Fifth Commandment, seniors, in terms of importance, are right up there with having no other gods, idolatry, revering the Lord's name, remembering the Sabbath, murder, adultery, theft, lying, and covetousness (Ex. 20). God must surely be thinking, "*What part of 'one of my highest priorities' do they not get?*" when He sees the low priority we all too often assign to seniors, as reflected by so many church budgets and ministry programs. Merely a "nice" thing to do? Hardly! It's more than that ... far more.

It's All Connected
The need for, as well as the value, importance and urgency of seniors ministry are each separate subjects worthy of their own chapter's worth of attention but are so inseparably connected that they require being treated together as one. Any one of them irresistibly implies the others. It's impossible to comprehensively address one without addressing them all. Where's the urgency, if the need isn't clearly understood? Similarly, how can one fully appreciate the importance without understanding the need or the value? Furthermore, unless there is a sense of urgency, even important matters of life can be assigned a secondary status until someday in the future. The sad reality is "someday" is no where to be found on anyone's calendar, weekly planner, or PDA (personal data assistant). I've yet to find churches that

budget time, energy, and resources for something that they may only get around to *someday*.

No Skipping Zone

If, before reading this book, you were already totally "sold" on seniors ministry, there may be a temptation to skip this first chapter, which focuses sharply on the importance of seniors ministry. If, on the other hand, you've picked up this book more out of curiosity or duty but are not seriously convicted about the importance of seniors ministry, there may be a temptation to skip over to chapter two. You may be more inclined to just "cut to the chase" and begin looking for sound-bite ideas and quick-fix formulas for seniors ministry. In both cases, let me urge you to resist such a temptation. In the first place, there are no quick fix solutions for providing exceptional seniors ministry. In the second place, one of the most important keys to developing an exceptional seniors ministry program in a local congregation is having a thorough understanding of the need for, as well as the value, importance, and urgency of seniors ministry.

Seniors ministry, unfortunately, is not usually an easy sell for a variety of illegitimate reasons (especially in a youth-focused culture). It's critical, then, to have thoroughly thought through the importance of seniors ministry before trying to encourage others to begin taking seniors ministry more seriously. Although seniors ministry is a delightfully gratifying ministry, it is so in a *different* way than other ministry efforts which are often perceived as more exhilarating. Trying to compare the emotional remunerative value of seniors ministry with other ministries is like trying to compare different good translations of the Bible. Some may personally prefer one over others but they're all equally valuable and equally essential in getting us to where God wants us to go. If we prefer one version over another, that's more of a commentary on us than upon another version. The point is, without a solid and in-depth grasp of the importance of seniors ministry, even the most well-intended will most likely rather quickly find themselves insufficiently prepared for the two-fold challenge that lies ahead. The first challenge involves encouraging and persuading churches as well as church leaders to begin treating seniors ministry more like a priority than an afterthought. The second challenge includes the task of persevering in your own personal senior ministry efforts without becoming discouraged from the lack of a supportive response that you may initially receive from others.

In our youth-focused culture with many other good needs and causes but with limited-resources, churches and church leaders aren't exactly "beating down the door" to begin taking seniors ministry more seriously. Odds are that any significant efforts you begin making to encourage churches and church leaders to take seniors ministry more seriously may be initially met with apathy or perhaps even resistance. Too many churches and church leaders are most likely "comfortable" with the low level priority they have relegated to seniors ministry. Seriously challenging them to

9

re-think God's priority for seniors in such a way that would result in any substantial changes to ministry programs and church budgets may be welcomed with open arms … or may be misperceived as a threat to the status quo. Although any opposition you may encounter will most likely be "passive-aggressive" in nature, it will be opposition just the same – which can be disheartening. Unless you have a firm grasp of the importance of seniors ministry, such apathy, resistance, and opposition can deter you from persevering.

"D & S" vs. "O & R"

We live a world that is very dependent upon dynamics and sensationalism. An expectation for the dynamic and sensational has so permeated our culture that it profoundly impacts every aspect of our lives – even when it comes to influencing our decisions about ministry efforts. If we're not careful, doing the right thing simply because it's the right thing to do can all too easily begin playing more of a *secondary* role in how we determine which ministry efforts churches decide to pursue the most energetically. Dynamics and sensationalism can overly influence how much priority is placed upon those pursuits - not that there is anything "wrong" with dynamic and sensational ministry. Our God is a dynamic God, well acquainted with doing sensational things in sensational ways. However, the same dynamic God who has been doing sensational things since before creation is the same God who also places a premium value upon the "ordinary" and the "routine." In fact, He seems to place an even higher value on what we usually perceive as the ordinary and the routine than He does on the dynamic and the sensational.

For example, the church in Corinth was so hung up on the dynamic and sensational experience of miraculous gifts that the Apostle Paul became quite emphatic about establishing the superior value of such "ordinary" things as faith, hope, and love (1 Cor. 12-14). When Jesus was people-watching at the temple one day and noticed a widow giving her meager two mites in the midst of other donations that dwarfed hers in comparison, Jesus valued the widow's contribution more (Lk. 21). At the end of their 70 years of Babylonian captivity, Zerubbabel led a band of captives from Babylon back to Jerusalem to begin rebuilding the temple. The people were discouraged because of the monumental task that lay before them but God, through the prophet Zechariah, chided them for discounting "*the day of small things*" (Zech. 4:10). Apparently, laying the foundation was not as exciting to them as building the walls. When the practice of some was to pray publicly in a charismatic way, Jesus placed a higher premium on simple, private prayer (Mt. 6:5f). When an omniscient God devised the way for conveying His message to the world, He chose to communicate that message in a way that the world would consider foolishness in comparison to flashier, intellectual arguments (1 Cor. 2:1f). In fact, when Jesus came into the world, God preferred a lowly manger over a regal entrance, and servanthood over worldly rule (Phil. 2:5-8).

10

When the tragedy of hurricanes Katrina and Rita were still fresh on everyone's heart, it would have been difficult to fathom not responding to such human suffering. The extraordinary outpouring of concern and sacrificial outreach was both inspirational and heartening. Generous Americans reportedly gave $700 million to the Red Cross and another $55 million to the Salvation Army within two weeks. Our government's response was estimated to have ranged somewhere in the billions ... not counting the millions of dollars from churches, individuals, and humanitarian organizations. Extraordinary human suffering usually evokes an extraordinary response.

Sometimes, human suffering and needs arise from natural disasters, (a hurricane along the Texas Gulf, an earthquake along the West Coast, a tsunami on the other side of the world). Other times, they are man-made (e.g. 9/11). But human suffering and need can (and routinely does) also occur in non-sensational and un "event" ful ways. These non-sensational events likewise deserve our equally extraordinary response - regardless of whether they arise from sensational or routine events of life. Suffering is suffering and need is need. We're not talking about measurable levels or degrees of severity but personal perceptions of pain. Although the scuffed knee of one child may not be as severe as the broken arm of another, suffering is suffering. Although a broken arm may be a more severe injury, as we measure severity of injuries, the child with the scuffed knee is no less wounded and traumatized than the child with the broken arm – from a personal suffering perspective. He also needs and deserves caring hugs and comforting kisses. He, likewise, needs and deserves our undivided time and attention, as well as whatever resources are required to bring comfort and healing just as does the child with the broken arm.

Our country's response to such tragic events, as mentioned previously, so clearly illustrates how much more enthusiastically we may tend to respond to human suffering born of *sensational* events than we do ordinary circumstances. Perhaps the reason God focused so much emphasis on seniors (as will be addressed in-depth throughout this chapter) is because He knew of our tendency to respond more enthusiastically to suffering that arises from sensational events than from non-sensational circumstances ... even though both are just as real to the sufferer and are equally deserving of our extraordinary response.

The ministry needs of seniors hurting from the loss of their home after a transition from independently living in the house that has been their home for the past 50 years into community living may never receive national media coverage. However, the loss to them is just as real and devastating as that of an earthquake victim whose house was reduced to rubble. The suffering of seniors who struggle with the loss of meaningful living in a youth-focused culture may never make the headlines, but their heartache is just as real as that of a hurricane survivor who has likewise lost hope to carry on. The suffering of seniors who have lost a spouse to age or disease, whether weeks, months, or years ago may never captivate the nation's undivided attention. The lingering wounds, however, are just as real to them as for those who still struggle years later with the loss of loved ones in the aftermath of 9/11.

Attempting to compare one kind of suffering as worse, greater, or more deserving of our extraordinary response is as misguided as trying to compare the worth and value of one life over another. Non-sensational suffering tugs at a loving God's heart every bit as much as does the sensational kind and it deserves our equally extraordinary response. When needs and suffering arise from sensational events, we need to express our sensitivity by responding extraordinarily with personal effort and individual pocketbooks ... and when it comes to the *non*-sensational needs and suffering that arise from the *non*-sensational events of seniors, our response should reflect an equally extraordinary response to their non-sensational ministry needs as well ... because suffering is suffering.

The importance of seniors ministry is not determined by dynamics and sensationalism. If the driving force behind our ministry efforts with seniors is more dependent upon dynamics and sensationalism than upon simply doing the right thing and honoring God's priority for seniors, we are building on a faulty foundation. We're building our ministry efforts with seniors upon a foundation that will likely sustain neither us nor the church that we may be encouraging to begin taking seniors ministry more seriously. It's only a matter of time before we will be disappointed and deterred from persevering in our efforts with seniors because seniors ministry is not about dynamics and sensationalism. Rather, it's about simply doing the right thing and honoring God's priority. Unless we have a thorough grasp of the high priority of seniors ministry, the rest of this book will likely have little of substantial value to offer. The need cannot be accurately assessed by dynamics and sensationalism. Rather, it is more accurately assessed from at least four different perspectives. There is the demographic perspective, the invisibility perspective, the mission perspective, and last but not least, there is the gold standard perspective.

A DEMOGRAPHICS PERSPECTIVE

From a demographics perspective, there are some astonishing statistics about the "graying" of America, due primarily to the "baby boomer" generation. According to statisticians, we are entering a unique time in American history. The year 2011, according to statisticians, will be a monumentally significant year of unprecedented proportions. It's the year a literal tidal wave of retiring baby boomers (those born between 1946 and 1964) begin crashing on the demographic shorelines of America in full force. In fact, the preceding ripples are already here. According to those who study such statistics, this growing number of retiring seniors will begin reaching critical mass very soon. It's been called a tidal wave by experts because that's what it looks like when graphed out on a timeline population chart.

According to experts in this field, there are some very revealing statistics about this massive group. There are somewhere between 76 and 84 million "boomer" seniors in America. Eleven thousand more boomers will be turning 60 years old every day. That's another senior about every 12 seconds - or over four million more each year! Furthermore, these figures fail to account for the older seniors of the "greatest generation" also among us. By the year 2011, the total number of seniors in America will begin reaching an unprecedented number in our country's history. This presents some logistical challenges for government programs, but more importantly, it presents both challenges and opportunities for churches and church leaders. The time to be laying the necessary foundation and building an adequate ministry support structure for a sufficient response is now! Shortsightedness will only leave us foolishly ill-prepared and seniors shamefully neglected.

The previously mentioned statistics as well as the additional ones below should serve as a wake-up call about the need to begin treating seniors ministry more like a high priority than an optional afterthought.

- The number of seniors 65 or older in the U.S. is rising twice as fast as the rest of the population.
- Seniors represent 1/3 of the entire U.S. population.
- There are more people in the U.S. over 65 than the entire population of Canada.
- Since 1983, there is a greater number of Americans over 65 than those under 25.
- Half of mainline Protestant church members are over 60.
- Americans 85 and older are the fastest growing segment in America today.
- Between 1960 and 1990, the 85 and older age group increased 232%.
- The 100 and older age group has doubled in the last ten years.

What Is And Is Not The Question

One thing is certain. This massive influx of seniors is coming whether or not we adequately plan and prepare for it. This statistical tidal wave is not subject to personal interpretation. Neither is it subject to sensational exaggeration or political "spin." It's a statistical fact, but it's not *just* a statistical fact. We're talking about living, breathing souls. We can either stick our collective heads in the sand, or we can begin preparing for this unprecedented tsunami of seniors that is imminently on the horizon. Either way, they're coming. The question is not will it or will it not happen. The question is not whether there will be a tidal wave of additional needs, challenges, and opportunities facing churches that come with these seniors. Needs don't "vanish" simply because one becomes older. Rather, needs often become greater. The only relevant question is really "*how many?*" How many seniors are we willing to overlook and underserve due to ignorance or apathy about the ministry

13

needs of seniors? How many opportunities are we willing to squander when it comes to utilizing the experienced skills and giftedness of this vast reservoir of individuals?

Our government is already bracing for the impact. It has concerns about how a significantly smaller number in the work force can possibly hope to sufficiently fund social security for so many seniors without raising taxes to levels that could give good cause for a second American Revolution. This imminent tidal wave is also one reason why, in recent years, there has been an effort on the part of government to seek and encourage additional faith-based solutions, rather than merely trying to rely upon "Uncle Sam" for everything. If even our government can see the handwriting on the wall about the challenges imminently ahead related to the graying of America, how can churches be so foolishly blind, underprepared, and negligent?

Wise and Foolish Virgins

How and *when* should God's people respond to this demographic tsunami of seniors headed into their retirement years? *How* congregations should respond is by *preparing* to meet their ministry needs and to utilize the opportunities this situation presents. *When* congregations should begin preparing for this situation is *now*. Jesus once spoke of ten wise and foolish virgins (Mt. 25). Five were deemed wise by Jesus because they planned and prepared ahead sufficiently for a significant and imminent opportunity. Another five, however, were declared foolish because of their blatant and deliberate disregard for preparedness. Consequently, they missed a marvelous opportunity. Significant, imminent events require sufficient, advance preparation, but the foolish wait until it's simply too late to avoid otherwise avoidable consequences.

Jesus used this analogy to establish a sense of urgency about a crucial matter He knew would be carelessly marginalized. Some were foolish, not because of a terribly foolish thing they *did*, but because of something they foolishly *failed to do*. They even had the example of others to follow (i.e. the five wise virgins). Similarly, it would be nothing less than foolish for churches and church leaders to knowingly ignore or even *marginalize* the urgent need to begin "trimming our lamps" in preparation for ministry with this phenomenally large number of seniors on the horizon.

The Clock Is Ticking

Seniors ministry in the 21st century is about preparing for the unique challenges as well as the marvelous opportunities that are actually already upon us and which will only become far greater in the very near future. Some of today's cutting edge leaders in seniors ministry say it could take at least three years for a congregation to develop an *exceptional* ministry program with seniors ... if that church is *seriously* focused on developing their seniors ministry efforts. Otherwise, it takes even longer! Informing, motivating, preparing, and equipping congregations *nationwide* makes the 2011 "deadline" even closer and the need to begin *now* all the more urgent. If the ministry needs of today's and tomorrow's seniors are to be met effectively and the opportunities utilized wisely, then visionary and innovative leadership among God's people cannot be postponed. Churches and church leaders must begin seriously developing their seniors ministry program *now*.

AN "INVISIBILITY" PERSPECTIVE

The need for exceptional seniors ministry should also be assessed from an invisibility perspective. Although the healthcare and housing needs of aging seniors may be evident enough, the *ministry* needs of seniors are typically not as evident and therefore are not given as much focus. This is especially true in comparison to the ministry needs of *younger* segments of the population. To blur our vision even more is our tendency to sometimes subconsciously substitute meeting *physical* needs with meeting *ministry* needs, when evaluating the *sufficiency factor*. However, this seems true only when it comes to seniors.

We readily see the value of providing children and teens with spiritual alternatives beyond having them merely sitting in the pew with the adults on Sunday mornings as was done in times past. Similarly, it's why we've also come to recognize the value of providing young and middle-age adults with alternatives beyond having them merely attending the auditorium adult Bible class on Sunday mornings. For the same reason, we must come to recognize the value of providing seniors with spiritual provisions beyond mere auditorium Bible classes, hospital visits, and an extra measure of moral support before, during, and after funerals. Seniors require the same kind of relevant, age-specific ministry efforts that more effectively address their other, more invisible ministry needs. If addressing the ministry needs of children and teens or young and middle-age adults requires more than classroom lessons with antiquated flannel graphs and traditional auditorium Bible classes from yesteryear, then addressing the ministry needs of today's seniors likewise requires more than predictable quarterly potlucks and seasonal gift baskets.

We must come to recognize the value of providing an *exceptional,* age-specific, and relevant ministry program for seniors within the church that will encourage and challenge their seasoned lives and tested faith. Programs and paradigms from the middle of the last century should be considered as unacceptable for today's ministry efforts with seniors as they would be for ministry efforts with today's children and teens, or young and middle-age adults. The ministry needs of seniors go far beyond food, clothing, housing, and medical care. Seniors, like all other age groups, have ministry needs that simply cannot be effectively addressed with minimal efforts aimed primarily at their *physical* needs. The needs of today's seniors (as will be addressed more extensively in chapter six) involve so much more than the basics of food, clothing, housing, and medical attention. Addressing their needs, like addressing the needs of children and teens or young and middle-age adults, requires so much more than a minimal effort that only addresses their physical needs.

15

A Disconnect

Unfortunately, there is often a "disconnect" when it comes to recognizing the other, more invisible ministry needs of *seniors*. When it comes to assessing the importance of ministry needs, the difference between our sensitivity for youth and for seniors is astonishing. The ministry needs of seniors simply aren't taken as seriously. The typical (though probably subconscious) mindset seems to be that when such basic needs as food, shelter and medical care have been provided for seniors, their needs have somehow been addressed, if not completely, at least sufficiently. Attention and resources given to seniors by federal, state, and local programs aimed at addressing their health and housing needs seem to give a false sense of sufficiency. It is a *false* sense of sufficiency because such programs focus on the *physical*, rather than on the other, more invisible *ministry* needs of seniors.

Apples and Oranges

Regardless of how unintentional it may be, we seem to have this "apples and oranges" perspective when it comes to seniors ministry. For example, even the numerous government programs that address the *physical* needs of teens seemingly don't distract or deter us from readily seeing the importance of addressing needs that go beyond their basic physical needs. I suspect, however, that because of numerous government programs for *seniors* we subconsciously think and feel that sufficient time, attention, and resources are already being devoted to seniors. Even though these programs are addressing their *physical* needs, they're *not* addressing the other, more invisible *ministry* needs of seniors. This "apples and oranges" mentality is most evident in the notable difference between the high priority we place upon youth ministry and the notably minimal effort we make with seniors ministry.

However, the other, more invisible ministry needs of seniors are no more sufficiently addressed (when addressing only "basic" provisions) than would the other, more invisible ministry needs of a child, a teen, or a younger adult be addressed when they've only received food, shelter, clothing, or medical care. All the many public and private sector programs that exist for seniors (such as Medicare and Medicaid, government housing programs, and long-term health care services at community living facilities) can unintentionally send a subtle but deceptive message of *false* assurance that seniors are getting their "fair share" of attention, which they may be for their *physical* needs. Medicare, Medicaid, and other federal, state, or local assistance programs go a long way toward addressing the basic *physical* needs of today's seniors. Senior community living centers and in-home assistance programs likewise go a long way toward addressing basic *physical* needs. However, the other, more invisible, *ministry* needs of seniors still need addressing. Government programs were neither designed nor intended to address the *ministry* needs of seniors.

When it comes to our ability to see the need for an exceptional ministry program for *seniors*, all these public and private sector programs for seniors seem to subconsciously have a dampening effect on us. In contrast, it seems to have no dampening effect whatsoever on our ability to see the need for providing exceptional *youth* ministry programs. Youth are by no means neglected by time, attention, and resources of either the public or private sector. There are innumerable federal, state, and local programs out there for youth (i.e. outside the realm of *church* efforts) like there are for seniors that address their *physical* needs for food, housing, and social activities.

The question that begs to be asked is why all these similar public and private sector efforts haven't seemed to deter us from seeing the importance of addressing the other, more invisible ministry needs of *youth*. We wouldn't dream of minimizing the importance or urgency of our youth ministry efforts and programs simply because of all these other public and private programs which are already in place for our youth. When it comes to youth, we can clearly see that they need far more than food, clothing, housing, and social activities. We likewise see that today's youth need so much more than what a mere "Bible class" or "church service" could ever hope to offer, but we seemingly fail to see it when it comes to seniors.

Some may rationalize that seniors already enjoy numerous opportunities for having their ministry needs met through church assemblies and Bible classes (as well as through occasional potluck dinners or periodic social outings). However, when it comes to meeting the ministry needs of *other* age groups, how many of us would use that same rationale for offering such a small amount of time, attention, and resources for youth ministry? Fortunately, we know better when it comes to *youth*. However, when it comes to *seniors*, we seem unresolved to make a similar high priority effort to encourage and challenge their seasoned lives and faith. For example, we wouldn't dream of considering mere access to church assemblies and Bible classes (or even pizza parties and occasional group trips to an amusement park) as sufficient efforts for meeting the ministry needs of today's teens. Rather, we hire full-time staff (thankfully!) and develop state-of-the-art programs (thankfully!) for our youth, so that we can offer them far more than merely sitting in a pew for Bible class and "church."

Seniors are people, too! Their needs require and deserve as much exceptional, age-specific time, attention, and resources as do our youth. The ministry needs of seniors are just as real as that of youth. We never reach a point of having no ministry needs simply by virtue of age. It's when we look at the needs of seniors through the eyeglass lenses of a youth-focused culture that we become color blind to their needs. We may know in a generic and poorly identified kind of way that seniors have needs, but when we look at them through the prism light of a youth-focused culture, we don't see the full spectrum of their needs.

If there were teens within a church or community whose *physical* needs were being neglected, caring churches and church leaders would eagerly reach out with

17

efforts to help provide food, temporary housing options, school supplies, and perhaps even some wholesome, social activities. At the same time, we'd also readily realize that teens have needs that go far beyond mere pizza parties, shelter, and occasional trips to an amusement park. We would readily understand that those teens also have *ministry* needs which are both important and urgent. When it comes to seniors, however, we seem far less capable of being consistent.

As we age, the appearance of obvious ministry needs may become more subtle. As a general rule, we can become more proficient and sophisticated at hiding those needs. However, the signs of unmet needs of seniors are clearly there for those who pay even half attention. From the adolescent to the teen to the young adult to the middle-age adult, there is a natural tendency to "act out" when needs are not being adequately met. The adolescent may begin misbehaving in school. The older teen may become rebellious and disrespectful of authority or perhaps begin dressing in bizarre ways. Young adults may struggle with relationships, while middle-age adults may have their "mid-life crises." However, when it comes to seniors, it is usually much different, or at least much easier to overlook or minimize their unmet needs, especially when we're not seriously focused on them anyway.

It's not that seniors don't also "send signals" when their needs are unmet. It's just that those signals may be more difficult to notice, especially to an inattentive youth-focused culture. Most seniors tend to indicate needs more through withdrawal and resignation. It's also less noticeable when seniors are already expected to step aside and become less engaged. In fact, judging from the comparatively small amount of time, attention, and resources devoted to seniors ministry, the implication would seem to be that seniors must essentially have little, if any, ministry needs beyond that of merely "attending church," being visited when ill or in the hospital, and perhaps having an occasional potluck fellowship.

With children and teens, we readily understand that when it comes to the basic provisions of life (food, clothing, and shelter) they still have other needs, which the basic provisions of life never begin to address. We recognize the value of such things as "quality time," family activities, and loving relationships on the *home-front*. We also recognize the value of having an exceptional, age-specific children and teen ministry program *within the church* that will encourage and challenge their tender faith. Similarly, most readily recognize that young and middle-age adults likewise have needs that extend beyond merely establishing careers, owning homes, and paying bills. They need to be encouraged and empowered to utilize their giftedness in service to others. They also need to be offered the kind of fellowship and accountability that comes from being a part of well organized ministry efforts of the church designed for them specifically. Consequently, we acknowledge the value of exceptional, age-specific ministry efforts within the church that encourage and challenge the developing faith of children and teens, as well as younger and middle-age adults. However, when it comes to seniors, we seem to think that their needs are already being met through the more generic adult activities being provided to members at large.

The Evolving Nature Of Needs

We never stop having needs. Rather, those needs simply change with time. To presume (even subconsciously) that one can reach a time and place in life where one has no needs is ludicrous. A baby, for example, may no longer have the need for diapers once he's potty trained, but that doesn't mean he no longer has any needs. An adolescent may no longer need a babysitter once he's old enough to be left alone for short periods of time, but that doesn't mean he no longer has any needs. A teen may no longer have the need for facial cleansers to fight pimples, once he gets past that stage of life, but that doesn't mean he no longer has any needs. A college student may no longer need to live at home and be dependent upon his parents once he graduates, but that doesn't mean he no longer has any needs.

Needs (whether physical, emotional, social, or otherwise) neither vanish nor suddenly cease simply because we've grown older. They can and often do change. The same is true with spiritual needs. Seniors may no longer have the need to learn how to fold their hands and "say grace" before a meal, but does that mean they no longer have any other ministry needs? Seniors may no longer have the need to "learn the books of the Bible" in class or at home. They may no longer have the need to "become active in the youth group" or go to "church camp" in the summer. They may no longer have the need to "date the right kind of person" to help ensure they marry someone who will be a spiritual helpmeet. They may no longer have the need to balance spiritual priorities with raising a family and making an income. They may no longer have these former needs but does that mean they no longer have any other ministry needs?

Seniors may no longer have the ministry needs of a child, a teen, a college student or a middle-age believer, but that doesn't mean they no longer have any ministry needs. Just like "church" and Bible class as they were done in the middle of last century are no longer sufficient for children and teens, or young and middle-age adults, neither should they be considered sufficient for today's seniors. The "apples and oranges" inconsistency that we have toward addressing the ministry needs of today's seniors is simply a silly rationalization for arbitrary preferences and subjective priorities. If we can recognize the changing needs of younger generations, it's not unreasonable to expect us to recognize that seniors are people, too, with evolving ministry needs just like everyone else. Seniors, likewise, require continued, pro-active, age-specific, time, attention, and resources.

We Usually Overlook What We're Not Looking For

One interesting characteristic of most people is that we tend to find that for which we're looking, but more significantly, we also tend to overlook that for which we're *not* specifically looking. Have you ever bought a new car or maybe merely added your dream model car to a future wish list, and "suddenly" you begin seeing that model car everywhere? It's not that there was a sudden influx of this particular model car on the road but rather that you simply began looking for it. We just have a tendency to find what we're looking for specifically. It happens all the time in life. We tend to look and listen for the needs of babies. Parents who take their infant seriously remain ever mindful of their precious child's needs and even *anticipate* those needs prior to any sign of need. For example, how many moms or dads have actually sniffed a diaper, even when the baby isn't crying - just to check? I've even seen moms poke their fingers down inside the diaper to check for wetness ... or worse. Wow! Talk about commitment to addressing unmet needs. We care so much that we not only want to *resolve* these needs, we even want to *prevent* them.

We're keenly aware of the needs of babies, regardless of whether or not there are any visible signs of distress. We also tend to not only address but even anticipate the needs of adolescents and young adults. Caring parents keep watchful eyes and ears out for even the slightest signs of trouble. They not only want to "nip it in the bud" (as ole Barney use to say on the Andy Griffith Show), they even want to prevent it, whenever possible. They do so by providing all kinds of wholesome, preemptive strike activities to fill the life of a child or teen. They want to help keep them out of trouble and on the right path. No caring parent would willingly allow an incident such as occurred at Columbine or Virginia Tech to occur through neglect. Hence, sports (such as baseball, basketball, soccer, or hockey) and numerous clubs or organizations (such as Boy Scouts, Girl Scouts, Brownies, Awana, or 4-H) are eagerly embraced and regularly utilized by parents.

The same is true with being aware of and meeting the *ministry* needs of younger generations. Many churches, for example, have state-of-the-art youth ministry programs, complete with highly organized, carefully planned, well funded, cutting edge ministry efforts led by a full-time specialist – often along with additional full-time, part-time, and volunteer staff. Many years ago, churches and church leaders finally began focusing on teen ministry. Now, many churches also have an equally strong emphasis on children ministry. Today's churches and church leaders would be considered out of touch, if not out of their minds, not to provide a state-of-the-art youth ministry program. We go out of our way to find and fill unmet ministry needs of our youth, while carefully, closely, and pro-actively looking and listening for signs of "problems." In fact, our objective is not to wait for problems to arise but to prevent as many as possible.

We consider the ministry needs of children and teens a high priority issue (as we should) and we eagerly address those ministry needs with utmost urgency (as reflected by enormous amounts of time, energy, attention, and resources devoted to it). Praise God for it! Churches and church leaders are to be commended for moving beyond the days when it was considered adequate and sufficient for children to merely sit on the pew with their parents and play with toys, eat cereal snacks, and draw on the visitors' cards while "listening" to the sermon. We more readily sense the importance and urgency of addressing the ministry needs of youth than we once did in the past. It's time for us to begin addressing the ministry needs of *seniors* more effectively and sufficiently.

"Where's Waldo?"

Another reason the ministry needs of seniors are not taken seriously enough is that if you're not proactively looking for their needs, you are not likely to see them, or you'll minimize them. It's extremely difficult to find what you're *not* looking for – even if it's right in front of you! Some of you may remember a picture puzzle years ago that was all the rave for a while. "Where's Waldo?" was the name of the game. For those who may be unfamiliar with it, "Where's Waldo?" was an extremely cluttered picture with "Waldo" hidden somewhere in the picture. Similar picture puzzle games have been designed for children, where you have to "find" certain objects carefully hidden on a page that have been cleverly camouflaged with the clutter of numerous other distracting things. In yet other similar picture puzzles, the object is to carefully scrutinize several *apparently* identical pictures and spot what's subtly different about one of them. The challenge of the "Waldo" game was to look very carefully until you finally found him. Failing to see the importance and urgency of seniors ministry reminds me of the old "Where's Waldo?" picture puzzles. The ministry needs of seniors can be right there before our eyes, and still we can miss seeing them because of all the "clutter" of other legitimate needs and worthy causes.

Let's take it a step further by *reversing* the situation. Imagine the likelihood of finding Waldo on the page, if we weren't even looking for him! The "catch 22" for churches, church leaders, and other believers, when it comes to seniors ministry, is that if we're not deliberately, intentionally, and proactively looking for the ministry needs of seniors, we are likely not to see them. If we don't *see* the ministry needs of seniors, we may never realize just how important and urgent it is to meet those needs. On the other hand, if we don't realize the importance and urgency of seniors ministry, why on earth would we even focus on looking for the ministry needs of seniors? It's a vicious cycle that must be broken. The very purpose and objective of this book is to help break that cycle of blindness, ignorance, and neglect. However, even this book, regardless of how helpful it may possibly be, still requires that we care at least enough to read it. This is why, if you're reading this book, you need to share its message with as many churches and church leaders as possible, and then engage them in meaningful discussion.

Seeing What's Not In The Picture

Discovering the importance of seniors ministry is apparently not something our youth-focused culture easily does. Several years ago, before I began seriously focusing on seniors, the ministry needs of seniors weren't exactly one of my high priorities either. Although I've "dabbled" in seniors ministry since my college days, seniors were not given the high priority I now realize I need to give them. As a freshman in college, I became part of a group of students on campus who, among other activities, visited "nursing homes" on a weekly basis. That's what everyone previously called them then, and how those who have updated neither their thinking nor their perceptions since the middle of the last century still perceive them. We visited these local nursing homes to sing and pray, as well as to provide short devotional messages for the residents. A few years later, a small part of my weekly ministry efforts for God still included visiting seniors. It wasn't until about 1999 that I began taking a much closer look at seniors ministry and more seriously re-evaluating their ministry needs. In fact, it was by "chance" (actually, it was a "God thing") that I even began focusing more upon seniors.

As one century was about to give way to another, I took that occasion to reflect deeply upon my life, its purpose, and the needs of others who were possibly being overlooked or underserved by churches and church leaders. The experience reminded me of "Where's Waldo?" only in reverse. As difficult as it is to look at a cluttered picture and find a cleverly hidden object, it's even far more difficult to look at that cluttered picture and see what *isn't* there. The more I studied the "picture" of all the many wonderful ministries, activities, and good works in which churches, church leaders, and other believers were engaged, the more it began to dawn on me that seniors ministry *wasn't* one of them. This spiritual "epiphany" about the need for exceptional seniors ministry was not inspired because I myself was a senior. I was only 46 at the time. Even now, by most standards, I'm not considered a "senior," although my grandson, as well as my graying hair, might suggest otherwise! It was a God thing. The more I stared into the "picture," asking God to reveal an area of need He wanted given more attention, the more seniors came into focus. Eventually, it became apparent that what God was clearly pointing at for me to "see" was what was *not* in the picture.

Conditioned From Birth

One more reason the ministry needs of seniors is not taken seriously enough is that everyone, whether he realizes it or not, is heavily and consistently conditioned from infancy onward not to focus on the needs of those older than himself. Crying babies are completely oblivious to the needs of their parents, even though those parents may be sleep deprived, out of work, ill, depressed, discouraged, lonely, out of money, or even preoccupied with the needs of that very baby's sibling! All a baby knows is that Mom and Dad can feed, change, hold, and comfort him. The needs of anyone older than the baby are irrelevant to the crying baby.

Elementary school children are likewise all but totally unaware of the needs of their parents. All they know is that Mom cooks meals for them to eat, as well as kisses and hugs away the pain of a "boo boo." All they know is that Dad is a "superman" who can do superhuman things that children can't do, such as driving them to the ball field for practice or a game, fixing their bike's flat tire, or protecting them from the "booger bear" during an overnight camping trip.

Teens, too, show relatively little awareness of the needs of those older than themselves. When there's a need for money, it's usually the teen looking to the parent, grandparent, or perhaps a close aunt or uncle for help, not the other way around. When they need to go to the doctor, it's the parent to whom they turn and on whom they rely. When there's a need for transportation, teens look to Mom and Dad for supplying the ride – or for asking their parents to loan them the car, complete with gas and spending money.

Once we're young adults, it's still our parents, or perhaps grandparents, to whom we most probably go for holiday meals. It is to them that we often turn for help with establishing our credit or buying that first house. As we reach mid-life, and as we struggle with raising our family and paying all the bills, we will likely find ourselves looking inquisitively toward *older* relatives for family genealogical background information. It is those *older* than we are to whom we look longingly, if not somewhat enviously presuming they have no needs. We see retirees and presume they have no mortgage payments. We envision them leisurely spending time on the golf course and in the flower garden, or at least merely "puttering around the house" in some relatively carefree lifestyle. We're conditioned from infancy to view those older than we are as having no needs, or at least as having needs that are neither as important nor as urgent as our own.

It's no wonder, then, that we have difficulty seeing the ministry needs of seniors. Given such lifelong and cultural conditioning, it's understandable *being* that way about seniors and seniors ministry. What is neither understandable nor acceptable is knowingly and willfully *remaining* that way. There is no acceptable reason for *remaining* ignorant, apathetic, and negligent about seniors ministry, especially once the importance of seniors ministry has been clearly brought to our attention. This is especially true when a specific "call" for exceptional seniors ministry has been made.

A MISSION PERSPECTIVE
A third way to more accurately assess the importance and urgency of seniors ministry (in addition to a demographic and invisibility perspective), is from a mission perspective. Although we know better, we tend to be much more focused on formation than *transformation*. By that I mean it would seem, emotionally speaking, that we're more into initial conversion than continual transformation. We get far more excited about sensational conversion testimonials than we do about the less

sensational task of incremental transformation. We live in a sensational world. The media make their living capitalizing upon it. Corporation products and services depend on sensationalism for company success and growth. Management relies upon it for motivating their sales force. Even churches prefer it hands down to the less sensational.

Who has ever seen or heard of a church promoting in the church bulletin, on the church sign out front, or during announcements before a church service, how Joe Member was slightly and non-sensationally transformed just a little more into the likeness of Christ this week? Instead, we prefer sensational testimonial about how God snatched someone from the fiery pits of hell and did some miraculous 180 degree turn with their life. It's not that we don't have an intellectual appreciation for the less sensational. It's just that it's not as emotionally captivating – and therefore doesn't draw the time, attention, and resources that we are eagerly willing to invest on other, more sensational ministry causes and efforts.

Incremental Transformation
The mission of the church, however, is at least as much about continual transformation as it is about initial conversion. In fact, a strong case could be easily made about continual transformation being far more important, given our Heavenly Father's ultimate objective. God's initial objective is to *save* us, but His ultimate goal is to incrementally *transform* us back into His likeness. The focus of the Great Commission is not upon conversion, but upon *discipleship*, which is a lifelong process consisting far more of the *non*-sensational than the sensational. Yes, discipleship includes conversion, but it's really only a small part of the process ... the beginning part.

Similarly, we're challenged not so much to be sensationally converted as we are to eventually *"be perfect"* or "full grown" as Jesus said (Mt. 5:48). God has given scripture to help make us "complete" – (i.e. incrementally full grown), as Paul explained to Timothy (2 Tim. 3:16), not merely initially converted. When the pressures of the world are continually trying to *"squeeze you into its mold,"* the antidote is not initial conversion, but incremental *transformation* (Rom. 12). When we look with unveiled face at the glory of the Lord, the intended benefit is not being merely converted, but being incrementally *"transformed from one degree of glory to another"* (2 Cor. 3:18). The mission of the church is very much about non-sensational nurturing and edification.

We understand the value and importance of non-sensational nurturing when it comes to family. As "sensational" as birthdays, vacations, holidays, and other special occasions can be, experts tell us that it's the routine, non-sensational things that matter most. What matters most are such things as daily hugs and pats on the back, bedtime stories, mealtime conversations, little words of encouragement and reassurance, the daily presence and consistent discipline of loving parents, and all the many other less than sensational activities of daily life. All these are just as valuable and important, if not more so, than all of the more sensational activities. The "mission" of the individual family is about so much more than the "sensational." The same is true with our *church* family's mission. This is why the need for, as well as the value, importance, and urgency of a seniors ministry program simply cannot be appropriately assessed from a dynamic and sensational perspective, as discussed in the previous section of this chapter.

Some church ministry efforts (the "popular" ones for which we spend the most amount of time, attention, and resources) are much like family birthdays, vacations, holidays, and other special occasions. They're fun, they're exciting, they're ... sensational. For example, to be a teacher for or to have an active part in a church's youth ministry program can be a very fun, exciting, and sensational experience. Likewise, those who have some active, leading role in a worship service led by a "praise team" can be very exhilarating and self-fulfilling. Leading a self-help or "12 step" recovery group, whether for alcoholics, parents of troubled teens, divorcees, abused spouses, or for financial advisement, typically offers a "spiritual high" for the one leading such noble ministry efforts. There is certainly nothing wrong with being involved with sensational ministry efforts, but the value of a ministry cannot be accurately assessed by how high it scores on the sensational meter. When Jesus taught the disciples about washing feet, its value wasn't determined by how fun and exciting or by how dynamic and sensational it was to do. The importance, value, and urgency of a ministry effort are best determined by the ultimate and only authority - God.

THE "GOLD STANDARD" PERSPECTIVE

A fourth way to accurately assess the importance and urgency of seniors ministry is from a "gold standard" perspective. Opinions differ when it comes to which ministry endeavors are worthy of a church's most serious time, attention, resources, and efforts. Personal preferences and priorities also change with time. In years past, churches have passionately pursued everything from door knocking to Vacation Bible School to bus ministries. In more recent times, everything from "Relief Efforts" to "Seeker Services" to "Leadership Training Workshops" has been effectively utilized. Each of these, as well as many other good ministry efforts, have (or had) merit and serve (or served) marvelous purposes. If, however, our bottom line objective is to please and honor God with our ministry efforts, we should look beyond mere cultural trends. We must likewise be sensitive to more than the changing personal preferences and subjective opinions of church members ... or even the preferences and opinions of church leaders that may change from decade to decade. We must be sensitive to God's explicitly stated, immutable priorities which transcend cultural trends and personal preferences, as well as time itself.

The Very Essence Of "Pure Religion"

One such ministry endeavor that transcends cultural trends and personal preferences is ministry with seniors. Unfortunately, seniors ministry is often little more than a footnote in too many church ministry efforts. It is often only a footnote even though scripture clearly distinguishes ministry with widows as one of only three causes that represents the "gold standard" for the very kind of endeavors God would have churches and individuals recognize as among His most basic and highest priorities (Jm.1:27). In additional to the emphasis of the 5th Commandment being reiterated by Jesus (Mt. 19:19) and Paul (Eph. 6:2), James also had some powerful input on the matter. In much the same spirit of the Decalogue, James summarized the very essence of *"pure religion"* in his epistle. In fact, James takes it a step further than the Decalogue. Instead of narrowing God's priorities down to *ten* items, he dares to narrow it down to *three (ministry with widows, ministry with orphans and personal purity)*. James' inclusion of widows once again elevates seniors to an incredibly high priority status in the eyes and heart of God.

Why does the Spirit compel James to distinguish widows so exclusively? Why would scripture call upon us to give such a ministry more than the nominal and obligatory nod it all too often receives today, as reflected in too many church programs and budgets? What is so distinctively "pure" about ministry with this category of believers that consists not exclusively but mostly of seniors? Things that are "pure" have one exclusive element, unlike a compound or an alloy. Gold jewelry that is merely 14 ct. is actually more utilitarily practical as jewelry and, therefore, more marketable because, in alloy form, it offers certain additional advantages, but it's not as distinctive as pure 24 ct. gold. Some good ministry efforts enjoy the advantage of serving more than one good purpose (which makes them more easily "marketable" to servant-hearted members). For example, youth ministry is not only a good thing to do; it's also popular within our culture. It builds future spiritual leaders, provides a positive alternative for kids, and offers spiritual help for parents. We have *multiple* incentives for pursuing youth ministry.

In contrast, the incentive for doing seniors ministry is "pure" because it's simply the right (godly) thing to do. As a rule, *"visiting senior widows in their distress"* will likely never enjoy the appeal or popularity of a vibrant youth ministry program in a youth-focused culture. Ministering to seniors will, likewise, not make those seniors future leaders for the next generation, although when younger generations participate in seniors ministry, it does help make future leaders out of such children and teens, as well as young and middle-age adults. Seniors also ordinarily need no positive alternative for staying out of the kind of trouble that children and teens often encounter. We will make ministry with seniors a high priority merely (i.e. "purely") because it's the godly thing to do. Since there are simply not the multiple (i.e. "alloy") incentives, we tend to treat seniors ministry as one of our lowest priorities. If believers are to discover and experience spiritual service in its "purest" possible form

... and if churches are to pursue ministry that *"God our Father accepts as pure and faultless"* – then we must re-think where seniors ministry fits into our priorities because it epitomizes God's gold standard for ministry in its purest expression.

Since at least the days of Moses, God has clearly demonstrated the high priority He has placed on seniors. Of all the things God had to share from His heart (from Genesis to Malachi and eventually to Revelation), God made a "Top Ten" list of His highest priorities – things that were nearest and dearest to His heart. God has never said an unimportant or insignificant thing, but on one occasion, He chose to narrow it way down and identify ten things that were even more important. Jesus utilized this same narrowing down concept when He spoke of *"weightier matters"* (Mt. 23) and *"greatest commandments"* (Mt. 22). Everything God has ever said is important. In fact, our very existence depends upon *every word* that proceeds from the mouth of God (Mt. 4:4). However, some things, according to God, are even more important.

Number Five and Number One

The Ten Commandments are actually two sets of God's highest priorities. The first four are "vertically" oriented, while the remaining six are more "horizontal" in nature. Of all the things God could have included in that highly select "short list" of things nearest and dearest to His heart (and therefore should be nearest and dearest to ours), our Heavenly Father included the fifth commandment about honoring fathers and mothers. Although the primary application may involve *parents*, the obvious broader application would include and implies honoring the elderly (i.e. parents do eventually and inevitably become older). Honoring fathers and mothers is as applicable a reference to *older* parents of adult children as it is to younger parents of teens. When it comes to God's intended relationship between younger children and their younger parents, the focal point is more upon the need for the child to *obey* his parents (Eph. 6:1). However, when it comes to God's intended relationship between *adult* children and their aging parents, the focal point seems to shift from obedience to *honoring*. Consequently, although the initial application of the fifth commandment may involve *parents*, the obvious broader application clearly implies and involves honoring *seniors*.

Upon even closer consideration, this list not only includes seniors as God's *fifth* highest priority, God also actually assigned them a *number one* priority status. When God began listing the second half of this highly select short list of His top ten highest priorities, parents (seniors) were at the very *top* of His horizontal list. The more you think about it, the more profound it becomes that God actually assigned them such a high priority. Of all the things He could have included in that highly select, short list of things nearest and dearest to His heart, God chose to include seniors. Given all that God has had to say to us, from Genesis to Malachi to Revelation, it's downright astounding. The Bible is actually a compilation of 66 books containing 1,189 chapters, 31,102 verses, and 788,280 words (1769 edition of the 1611 KJV). Of all

27

the many important things God wanted to share in all these many chapters, verses, and words, He wanted to make it especially clear to us what was the *most* important among all those important things He chose to say. Seniors were included in that short and exclusive list. Wow!

Highlighters, Red Pens, and Asterisks

When I read a book, I always read it with a yellow highlighter. By the time a book is published, it has already survived the numerous revisions of the writer, as well as input from trusted friends and colleagues. Then, there's the editor who "bleeds red ink" all over it. By the time a book is actually published, it is presumably in its most concise and cogent form. Presumably, all the irrelevant and insignificant "fluff" has been removed. All that should be left is the most important of all the important things the author has to share. Although at this stage everything written by the author would now be considered absolutely essential to include, there are still some things the author says that are more important than other things – hence, the reader's use of a yellow highlighter.

When God makes the effort to create a "top ten" list within His word, that's essentially equivalent to God smearing yellow highlighter all over it (and maybe also underlining it in red, along with an a few asterisks in the margin). We'd be wise to pay very special attention, not from a legalistic "gotcha" do-list perspective, but from a sensitive-to-what's-important-to-God perspective. If it's that important to God (i.e. important enough to place it in such a highly select, top priority list), then it ought to be that important to us. It ought to be that important, not out of obligation, but out of love and respect for being of one mind, heart, and soul with God. It ought to be that important to us because we long to share in, and be partakers of, His divine nature (2 Pet. 1:4).

Some might quibble about how much or even whether the 5th commandment can be applied to seniors ministry. Admittedly, the primary meaning is about parents, but an obvious secondary application includes seniors. To deny such application is to become dangerously close to the same legalistic technicalities of the Pharisees, who quibbled over this very verse, using a practice called corban in order to "Kings X" their way out of the obvious spirit and full intent of God's explicitly stated priority. To insist that the fullest meaning intended or that the only legitimate application that can be made from the 5th Commandment is strictly and only about *young* parents of young children - and cannot have any secondary application for honoring seniors is just silly. The high priority status of seniors, however, is not dependent on the Decalogue to substantiate this high priority of God's - far from it. The evidence of God's high priority for seniors (and seniors ministry) is not contained in simply one "proof text." Rather, it's revealed in an accumulative way. God has made His priority for seniors known in other ways, too.

The Least Of These

Although God has made it abundantly clear elsewhere in scripture that we are saved by His grace and not by our own merit (Eph. 2:8, Tit. 3:5, etc.), He also takes note of how and whom we serve during our time on earth. He apparently has a special appreciation for how (and if) we serve those who are *"the least of these"* among us. No doubt, God is both pleased and honored with whomever we serve, but He seems *especially* pleased and honored when we focus our attention on the "underdogs" of life - the thirsty, the hungry, the estranged, the poorly clothed, the sick, the imprisoned (Mt. 25). In fact, He takes it quite personally – so personally that when we've ministered to such individuals, He says we've ministered to Him.

Jesus was continually surrounded by crowds wanting a "piece of Him" to be healed or helped in one way or another. This was apparently rather worrisome for His disciples who at times felt compelled to act as personal "bodyguards" for Him. On one occasion, the pressing crowds must have been especially annoying to them because scripture says, *"Then were there brought to him little children, that He should lay His hands on them and pray"* (Mt. 19:13, 14). Mark's version says, *"They were bringing to Him children"* (Mk. 10), implying that they just kept continually coming in droves and by wave after wave after wave. Luke's version adds yet another dimension to the situation, calling these children babies (Lk. 18).

How incredibly different Jesus' perspective of ministry was from that of His disciples. What the disciples saw was a crowd of unimportant (or at least less important) people taking up and taking away valuable time and energy from Jesus, who had more important things to do than fool with an endless array of the snot-nosed kids and whining babies of a bunch of near hysterical parents. Jesus, however, had a far different perspective, tenderly reprimanding them by saying, *"Freely allow the children to come to me. Stop preventing it" (Lk. 18).* Then, Jesus takes it yet a step further, essentially stating, *"These are my kind of people."* Whereas the disciples saw little value in devoting time to "the least of these" kind of individuals, Jesus was saying that's what kingdom service is all about, from His perspective. It's the very essence of kingdom work.

God, through the ages, has always been especially attentive to the needs of the underdogs of life. The steady drumbeat of God's special concern for those most especially vulnerable to "falling through the cracks" because of their "least of these" status in life can be clearly heard throughout scripture. Historically, God has placed a special priority status on such individuals as *the stranger, the fatherless, and the widows"* – whether that involved allowing them to freely glean any remaining valuable crops from the fields of others (after the first harvest) at neither cost nor repercussions (Deut. 24:19f), respecting their personhood rather than taking advantage of them just because one could (Ex. 22:22), proactively tending to their needs rather than neglecting them (Deut. 10:18,19), bearing avoidable losses rather

29

than selfishly misrepresenting circumstances about them to your own advantage (Deut 27:19), discouraging them (Job 31:16), and so forth. God cares for everyone, but He has historically always been *especially* mindful of "the least of these" among us ... which surely includes aging seniors.

If seniors are that important to God, why do so many church budgets and programs reflect them as so *un*important? Isn't it amazing how we've reached the point that what's *most* important to God seems *least* important to us? I suspect any honest appraisal of our ministry efforts and church budgets would all too clearly reveal that seniors and seniors ministry are a very low priority. In fact, I'm not sure it would be accurate to even call them a low priority, because even a low priority still enjoys the status of being a priority, even if it's a low one. In our youth-focused culture, seniors and seniors ministry would seem to rate quite below even a low priority status. Rather, it would seem all too clearly that seniors ministry is far more of an obligatory or token afterthought than even a low priority.

Several years ago, I knew of a rather large, active, and growing church that had numerous good works happening. I had the occasion to look at their annual budget, which revealed that they dedicated $10,000 per week for youth ministry efforts, while for seniors ministry they devoted a mere ... $56. No, that's not a "typo" or a misprint. It's just the tragic truth. This is not to "pick on" any particular church. This gross disparity only typifies our general mindset and practice when it comes to how much (i.e. how *little*) we value seniors and seniors ministry. As the old axiom suggests, if you want to know where someone's priorities are, just follow the money. Jesus said it this way, *"Where your treasure is, there also will be your heart"* (Mt. 6:21). The sad reality is that we have far too little heart for seniors and seniors ministry. As harsh and judgmental as that may sound, what other conclusion is feasible, when you're looking at the inequity reflected by $10,000 vs. $56? God has a heart for seniors and ministry with seniors. That's *His* perspective. It should also be ours. Seniors are one of His highest priorities. They should be ours too.

Stuck In The Past

When talking about the importance of ministry with today's seniors, it is also necessary to make a distinction between old and new paradigms. Just as ministry efforts with today's youth have changed paradigms since the middle of the last century, so must our ministry efforts with today's seniors. When we think about *youth* ministry, we don't think about replicating or perpetuating how it was done in the 1950s. Rather, we're always on the hunt for newer, better, more effective ways to go about it ... even a new paradigm approach. In order to be effective with today's *youth*, we know we can't remain stuck in the past. It should be no different with *seniors* ministry. In order to be exceptional with today's seniors, we simply cannot remain stuck in the past.

The good news is - there is a new and better paradigm way to do seniors ministry! The not so good news is – we still have an old paradigm approach toward ministry with seniors that has been left over from the middle of the last century. Even churches that are stepping up their efforts are often only pouring the new wine of a few additional "activities" into the same old wineskin of an outdated paradigm perspective. Just as the time came for the Old Covenant of Moses to give way to a new and better one, the time has come for a new paradigm for seniors. Just as the time came for ministry with youth as it was done decades ago to give way to a newer, better way as is being done with today's youth, the time has come for us to make a similar paradigm transition in ministry with seniors. What, though, does that new paradigm look like, and how does it differ from the same old paradigm efforts that have been going on unchanged for at least the past half century? There are several distinctive differences.

What Does A New Paradigm Look Like?

One distinctive difference between the old paradigm and a new paradigm of seniors ministry is the motivational basis behind even doing it. Determining the importance of providing exceptional ministry with today's seniors is neither measured nor determined by the audible outcry of seniors but rather is determined by the outcry of God on behalf of seniors. We will likely never see the need for a more effective, new paradigm approach to seniors ministry if we wait for seniors to begin demanding more time, attention, and resources for themselves. Generationally speaking, it's just not their "style" to be so self-focused. They'll suffer silently from neglect. Perhaps worse, they'll live in denial of their own ministry needs, rather than make demands upon their home church for an exceptional seniors ministry program. Neither will there likely ever be a compelling outcry within the congregation by enough others on their behalf – not in a youth-focused culture.

Furthermore, we must dig deeper than anecdotal evidence for an incentive to begin taking seniors ministry more seriously. Anecdotal evidence (derived from superficial surveys and impersonal polls) is neither sufficient nor reliable, especially when it comes to assessing the importance of seniors ministry. In other words, merely polling the congregation for their opinion about or interest in seniors ministry is simply insufficient if you're *seriously* interested in finding and meeting the ministry needs of seniors. Even polling seniors themselves is unreliable because superficial polls and surveys can no more sufficiently reveal the ministry needs of seniors than can superficial polls and surveys reveal the ministry needs of anyone else.

Seniors are particularly disinclined to broadcast their ministry needs anyway. They certainly won't "spill their guts" in some superficial, check-list survey. Rather, they're more likely to do without or even suffer silently than whine or pronounce demands for themselves. So, if seniors will not speak up for themselves and neither will enough others, then God's voice is the only convincing one seniors really have

31

but all that should be required. If we come to an understanding of the need for, as well as the value, importance, and urgency of ministry with today's seniors, we will "get it," not because of feedback derived from superficial surveys, but because we become more sensitive to divine priorities than we are to mortal preferences, mere opinions, and anecdotal evidence.

A second distinctive difference is that churches and church leaders with a new paradigm perspective will enthusiastically embrace and endorse, as well as publicly promote exceptional seniors ministry. They will recognize all the "corban" excuses for what they are and begin thinking, planning, and moving beyond all the "ifs," "ands," or "buts'" in order to focus their undivided attention only upon the "how." Churches and church leaders with a new paradigm of seniors ministry simply stop with all the excuses - regardless of limited funds and tight budgets ... regardless of a roof or an AC that may soon need replacing ... regardless of how helpful another wing to the building would be ... regardless of more parking area that may need paving ... regardless of the need for additional staff personnel for other ministry efforts ... regardless of the genuine need for responding to some unexpected natural disaster, whether locally or elsewhere. They simply stop with any and all the excuses or even the "reasons" and simply *find* a way ... *regardless*.

They *find* a way, even if it requires restructuring their budget, taking up a special contribution, or making a cooperative effort with area or sister congregations. The problem is rarely money, anyway. It seldom ever has been. The *real* problem is a lack of vision and resolve, accompanied by a resistant attitude – a passive aggressive resistance against taking seniors ministry seriously. Admittedly, making any transition from a comfortable and familiar, but outdated and less effective old approach to a new and more effective one is never obstacle free or without challenges. Seldom are any endeavors that honor God's higher priorities.

A third difference is that seniors ministry will be treated as its own "stand alone" ministry - neither subordinate to nor merely an extension of some other "primary" ministry. Meeting the ministry needs of today's seniors sufficiently and effectively requires the same kind of focused time, attention, and resources that is usually made available for ministry efforts that are considered a "main" ministry of the church. In fact, one of the clearest indications of an old, outdated paradigm perspective of ministry with today's seniors is when we place seniors ministry *under* our benevolence program. Such an organizational arrangement is out-of-touch thinking left over from a time when ministry with seniors was viewed as consisting of little more than occasionally paying the utilities, buying food for, or covering the monthly house note of some poor widow during difficult times.

Imagine if we approached youth ministry in the same way we do ministry with seniors. What if youth ministry was merely subordinate to or merely a minor extension of, say, "miscellaneous outreach?" How effective would we be with meeting the ministry needs of today's youth if we only gave them our *minimal* time, attention, and resources as is too often done with today's seniors? Merely providing occasional potluck socials for seniors would be equivalent to merely handing out pizza coupons and video games to teens. Merely providing seniors with periodic bus trips to the art center or museum would be equivalent to merely taking teens as a group to the movies or an amusement park. We must adopt a completely different paradigm toward seniors ministry. It should be one that treats seniors ministry as a "primary" ministry effort. It should not relegate seniors ministry to a secondary or worse status. Exceptional seniors ministry deserves and requires being more than merely a sub-part of some other primary ministry.

A fourth distinctive difference between the old and a new paradigm of seniors ministry is that seniors and seniors ministry are *intentionally* promoted with a new and positive image, as will be discussed in greater detail in chapter four. Sadly (and unnecessarily!), public perception of seniors and seniors ministry is not only less than positive, it's often downright unappealing and uninviting – even to seniors. Seniors ministry, quite frankly, is in desperate need of a public image "makeover." This makeover is not needed in order to deceptively place some gimmicky, positive "spin" on an otherwise inherently negative thing. Rather, it's needed to publicly educate congregations in order to more closely realign the church's *misperception* of reality with God's *actual* reality of a *positive* perspective of seniors.

A high profile effort must be persuasively presented to establish this new and positive image of seniors and seniors ministry. We must stop unwittingly allowing seniors ministry to be treated as little more than some second class cause only worthy of a "B" team effort. Seniors and seniors ministry should be proactively promoted as a positive thing until the church's public perception changes. This will not just "happen." It will take a deliberate effort of thoughtful planning, determined persistence, visionary leadership, equitable resources, and enthusiastic creativity to establish this new and better vision.

A fifth distinctive difference between the old and a new paradigm is that those engaged in seniors ministry will think, plan, and act in ways that work toward regularly integrating seniors with (rather than usually segregating seniors from) other generations in activities of fellowship and service. The new paradigm envisions *inclusion*, rather than exclusion. Seniors ministry is not just about seniors. It's about teens and children, as well as college and middle-age adults, engaging in intergenerational activities of fellowship and service on a regular basis (i.e. beyond Bible classes and "church"). Otherwise, seniors ministry too easily becomes stigmatized as little more than an "old folks social club" in which seniors prefer not to associate themselves because of the stereotypically negative connotation attached to aging. Excessive age segregation can also unintentionally, as well as unwittingly, promote a patronizing attitude toward seniors. Such an atmosphere encourages sympathetic, disdainful coddling more than meaningful, purposeful *co*-fellowship and *mutual*-ministry efforts. Ministry with today's seniors should be very much about seniors discovering ways to remain useful to God and relevant to younger generations around them.

A sixth difference between the old and a new paradigm is that seniors ministry is as much about developing opportunities for seniors to serve as it is about meeting their needs. Those with an old paradigm view of seniors ministry think mostly in two-dimensional black and white. They think primarily in terms of older members with declining health in need of an occasional visit and some passing words of encouragement. Old paradigm thinking is more the scratching of an obligatory itch with *minimal* effort than an exceptional effort. In contrast, the new paradigm envisions promoting and developing opportunities for seniors to serve in age-specific ways that are especially appealing and particularly meaningful to seniors. The new paradigm encourages and challenges seniors to find their place of service. This is done with the help of leaders who with intention, inspiration, and creativity help innovatively envision, thoroughly identify, and energetically utilize the seasoned giftedness of their senior members.

This new paradigm publicly abandons the "retirement" image stereotypically associated with seniors and *raises* the bar of expectation for seniors and seniors ministry. If we approached youth ministry like we typically do seniors ministry, there would be no such thing as summer work camps or periodic service projects that challenge teens to become less self-focused on their own wants, needs, and problems. If we did youth ministry like we do seniors ministry, church attendance and social activities are about all that youth would be expected and encouraged to do. Just as effective youth ministry inspires, challenges, and leads our youth to discover their own unique, age-specific ways and places to serve, ministry with today's seniors should do no less.

One final distinctive difference between the old and a new paradigm of seniors ministry is that in multi-staff sized churches, seniors ministry becomes someone's *full-time* effort. Admittedly, depending solely upon a very loosely organized coalition of spontaneous volunteers casually and occasionally coordinated without someone's undivided attention may be all that is needed when all we envision for seniors ministry is a minimal and mediocre effort. However, those with a new paradigm who seek to be as exceptional with seniors as we are with youth require someone's full-time attention.

Some ministries lend themselves well to part-time attention and volunteer leadership, but exceptional seniors ministry isn't one of them. Again, imagine pursuing ministry with today's youth as half-heartedly as we pursue seniors ministry.

How effective would we be with youth if we depended only upon a loosely organized coalition of volunteers? How effective would that ministry effort be if it were led *without* someone's undivided attention? How effective would that ministry program be if efforts seldom seriously addressed other, more invisible ministry needs of our youth?

The importance of exceptional seniors ministry is clear for those who are willing to see it from God's perspective. Seniors are people, too! They have ministry needs just like everyone else. God has even highlighted His high priority for them in scripture. The sooner we begin seeing seniors ministry through the eyes of God, instead of through the eyes of our own personal preferences, the sooner we will be compelled to develop a newer, better perspective and then begin applying a new paradigm that will result in *exceptional* ministry with today's seniors.

CHAPTER TWO

The North Star
(core values for exceptional ministry with seniors)

Whether or not a mission statement is formally and officially created, it would be wise to at least establish clearly in your mind what your objective is whenever beginning or expanding any seniors ministry efforts within your home congregation. This is best done by going through the process of actually creating a mission statement, along with some core values, which can serve as guidelines for goals and objectives. The more specific and intentional we can be about our objective the more exceptional we can become in our efforts. Establishing a mission statement, along with some core values, is much like laying a solid foundation before building a structure. Jesus affirmed the importance of building a house on a solid foundation. He also spoke of the foolishness of proceeding with a building project or going to war without first counting the cost. You may find the following mission statement and core values helpful to jumpstart your thinking. Following the mission statement and list of core values are some additional thoughts about each.

MISSION STATEMENT

"Sage Ministries is committed to treating seniors ministry more as a priority than an afterthought by equipping and empowering congregations with the tools, training, and motivation helpful for providing exceptional ministry with today's seniors while also challenging seniors to discover meaningful opportunities to serve."

There are several key components to developing an exceptional seniors ministry effort, as revealed in the above mission statement. One is serious *commitment*. We already have plenty of *half-hearted* efforts at seniors ministry. We don't need any more. There are already too many seniors ministry programs that take more of an *afterthought* approach toward seniors ministry. What seniors need are churches and church leaders who are irrevocably resolved to begin providing exceptional rather than mediocre ministry with and for seniors.

A second key component to this mission statement is equipping and empowering. The old adage, *"Give a man a fish and feed him for a day, but teach a man to fish and feed him for a lifetime,"* could not be more applicable than when it comes to exceptional seniors ministry. The needs are too many and the number of seniors is too vast for only one person or even a small handful of people to establish an exceptional seniors ministry program. One person reaching out to a few seniors is a good start, but only a start. Exceptional seniors ministry requires equipping and empowering as many others as possible to do the same.

A third key component in this mission statement includes challenging seniors to serve. Seniors ministry is at least as much (if not more so) about seniors serving others as it is about having their own ministry needs met. There is still a place of meaningful service in God's kingdom for seniors to serve – even among those who may not be as active and healthy as in their younger years. They must, however, be faithfully encouraged, challenged, and led by an exceptional seniors ministry program.

CORE VALUES

Below is a list of core values that serve as guiding principles for Sage Ministries. Perhaps they will be useful in helping establish some guidelines for exceptional seniors ministry in your home congregation. This is not, however, some "secret formula" to success that will just happen. These core values no more magically work themselves than does the greatest diet program in the world work itself. Just like you have to actually work a diet if you want the diet to "work," you have to actually work these core values if you want these core values to "work." Please also note the action verbs that begin each core value – addressing, appreciating, discovering, involving, recognizing, effectuating, affirming, exchanging, fostering, challenging, reflecting, equipping, and empowering.

Core Value 1
Addressing the unmet and sometimes "invisible" ministry needs of today's seniors

As mentioned earlier in chapter one, seniors are people, too, with ministry needs just like everyone else. The needs of seniors, however, are often "invisible" … or at least less obvious. For example, August 15, November 4, and every Friday evening are three days of "invisible needs" for my mother. The first is my deceased dad's birthday, to whom my mother was married for 52 years. The second is their wedding anniversary. I say "is" because those dates and days haven't mysteriously vanished from the calendar simply because my dad passed away nearly a decade ago. The third is "family night" (when my brother and I were children). "Invisible" needs, however, consist of so much more than days on a calendar. Other invisible needs might include locations, sights, sounds, and even smells that set off memories that could trigger sadness or loneliness. Invisible needs could arise from watching a movie, reading a book, or hearing of some current news event. Regardless of what causes the invisible ministry need, the point is, invisible ministry needs exist. In fact, they surround seniors on a daily basis, as they do individuals at any age. If seniors ministry in a church isn't taken seriously, there will be many, many invisible ministry needs that go continually unmet among seniors.

Core Value 2
Appreciating the experienced skills and wisdom of seniors

Seniors – especially spiritually mature seniors - have accumulated a lifetime of skills, experience, and wisdom that is not only valuable to continue utilizing, but is also worth blessing others with by sharing. In our rush-rush world with a disposable mindset, younger generations must learn to appreciate - genuinely and authentically *appreciate* the value of what seniors have to offer. Younger generations have an opportunity to benefit from the skills, experience, and wisdom of seniors, but it will take a "whole 'nuther" way of looking at seniors and what they still have of value to offer others. It's likewise a mutually beneficial relationship. Seniors, when sincerely asked to share their skills, experience, and wisdom with others, have an opportunity to continue being useful, as well as an opportunity to continue feeling and *being* needed. However, two essential things must happen. First, seniors must exchange a "retirement *from*" perspective for a "retirement *to*" outlook. Second, *non-seniors* must likewise abandon this destructive "retirement from" view of seniors and become proactively open and receptive to interacting with and learning from seniors.

Core Value 3
Discovering the place of meaningful service seniors still have in the kingdom

Seniors, especially once they've entered the "retirement" years of their life, often struggle with maintaining or rediscovering meaning and purpose in their life. For women, this could begin setting in as soon as the kids move from home, initiating the "empty nest" stage of life. For men, it more likely centers on retirement from their career. Helping and encouraging seniors to remain useful in service to others is key for seniors to continue living a life with meaning and purpose.

Core Value 4
Involving individuals of all ages who care about seniors

Seniors ministry is not just about seniors. The more this core value principle is applied, the more exceptional our ministry efforts will be with seniors. Seniors ministry should be an intergenerational effort. It certainly should involve seniors serving seniors, but an exceptional seniors ministry program also includes and involves others of all ages, from middle-age adults, to young adults, to college students, to teens, and even children. All generations are involved in serving seniors and in serving side by side *with* seniors. In fact, some of the most powerful ministry that can occur with seniors is through children. Few things can bring a smile on the face of seniors more quickly than for them to be in the presence of a child. An exceptional effort, then, involves younger generations serving seniors and serving with seniors in a *mutual* effort.

Core Value 5
Recognizing the ministry needs of caregiving adult children of aging seniors

Any comprehensive approach to seniors ministry must include being supportive toward caregiving adult children of aging seniors. More and more adults, who may not yet even be seniors, are finding themselves "sandwiched" between the responsibilities and obligations of still raising their own family and the need to begin more proactively caring for their aging parents. Such double duty responsibilities can become both exhausting and overwhelming. This can be especially difficult when adult children and their aging parents are living in different cities or states. This can create an additional strain on an already challenging situation. Resolving this long distance gap (moving them closer or having them live with you) may provide some relief but it doesn't make it a stress free situation. In fact, it could increase the stress level. It, likewise, doesn't eliminate the need for encouragement that best comes from an exceptional seniors ministry program.

Core Value 6
Effectuating and reinforcing a more positive and beneficial image of seniors

Let's be honest and lay all "Politically Correct" pretentiousness aside. Seniors, in our youth-focused culture, have a negative image. They've been stereotyped and saddled with a bad reputation. Some may have earned that negative image … but only some, not all. Those who did earn it earned it because of their personal character, not because they are seniors. Someone once wisely said that seniors don't become cranky because they are seniors. They just become "more so." Who they've always been just becomes more and more pronounced and obvious with age. As a rule, a sweet, kind, loving, spiritually minded individual will most likely become a sweet, kind, loving, spiritually minded senior.

"Ageism" (like racism, sexism, and most other "isms" of the world) is wrong, as well as unfair and hurtful. Martin Luther King boldly championed for the day when an entire race of people would be judged not by the color of their skin but by the content of their character. Churches, church leaders, younger generations, and even seniors themselves need to begin championing for the day when seniors are judged not by the age of their body or number of candles on a cake, but by the content of their character. However, this public relations makeover will require an intentional and persistent effort on the part of churches, church leaders, and seniors, as well as other members who care about seniors.

Seniors, by their daily living as well as by their very attitude and outlook on life, need to set a high standard for themselves as mentors who are truly worthy of emulation from younger generations. Younger generations, by their actions as well as by their words, need to *demonstrate* the value they see in seniors and not merely pay lip service to it. Both seniors and younger generations need to become aware of and sensitive to degrading attitudes and practices that only propagate and perpetuate a negative image of seniors. They need to discourage such attitudes and practices as jokes about being old (i.e. black balloons at 30 or 50) or demeaning language ("my old man"). Notice I didn't say "ban" such attitudes and practices in some legalistic manner, but rather become aware of and be personally offended by them. *Racism* shouldn't have to be "banned" to be eliminated, especially when it comes to churches, church leaders, and all other believers. It should just be personally and instinctively offensive out of respect for every individual. Similarly, *sexism* shouldn't have to become some law or rule that requires enforcing by some "spiritual Gestapo." Rather, it should be that we have no heart for treating any individual more as an object than a person. The same is true concerning *ageism*. For the believer, ageism shouldn't have to be "outlawed" to be eliminated among God's people.

Core Value 7
Affirming the purpose, significance, and relevancy of seniors

Everyone needs and deserves affirming. *Children* need affirming while they're young and struggling to learn the "three R's" in school. *Teens* need affirming as they're trying to grow up and while they're struggling with complexions and peer pressure. *College students* need affirming as they begin struggling to handle their newfound freedom and independence without abusing the one and losing the other. *Young adults* need affirming while still finding their way in the midst of struggling with interviews, career limitations, and starting a family. *Middle-age adults* need affirming as the ever-increasing weight of life's responsibilities begins to take its toll while they struggle with the various forms of "mid-life crisis" in their life.

Seniors need affirming, too! Once seniors begin experiencing the empty nest – once they leave the workforce - once they begin developing chronic health conditions – once they begin finding themselves more out of the loop than in the loop of their former co-workers, their children, and even their home church, they need affirming more than ever. When children are no longer depending on us - when business associates are no longer counting on us - when churches are no longer relying on us, we can lose sight of having a purpose for life. When we no longer seem to "matter," we can feel incredibly insignificant and irrelevant.

Core Value 8
Exchanging past success for present purpose, significance, and relevance

Seniors need to be *verbally* affirmed about their continued purpose, significance, and relevancy. They also need to be *empowered* for it. It's simply not enough for them to merely *hear* it. They need to *experience* it. In fact, mere verbal affirmation without empowerment will more than likely ring hollow and sound more like condescending patronization than authentic affirmation. One of the best ways to help a senior *feel* he still has a life with purpose, significance, and relevance is to help him *live* a life with purpose, significance, and relevance. In a youth-focused culture in which seniors are expected to retire, step aside, and get out of the way, it takes empowerment to help seniors maintain a meaningful life. Like the unemployed professional whose previous job position has been outsourced or phased out, seniors may need to "re-tool" to remain useful.

This may require additional schooling, or it may involve finding new or different applications for the skills they already have to offer. Exceptional seniors ministry will encourage seniors to re-tool for ministry and will empower them to find new ways to apply themselves for service in God's kingdom. Seniors cannot live in the past, but they can use that past for maintaining purpose, significance, and relevance for the present and the future.

Core Value 9
Fostering intergenerational friendships and fellowship

Seniors ministry is not just about seniors. When Paul encouraged the *"older women to teach the younger women"* (Tit. 2), he was recognizing the mutual value of intergenerational friendships and fellowship. Godly seniors, whom God has spent a lifetime shaping, molding, and transforming, have much to offer younger generations in the form of wisdom and experience. Like a fine wine or seasoned wood, some things just take time. New wine simply cannot offer the "character" of a finely aged wine. Nothing burns as warmly as wood that has been "seasoned" with time. This same time advantage is also inherently true about godly seniors. All the genetics and education of the world still cannot offer what only time has to offer to others from those who have been "aged" and "seasoned" by the Spirit for a lifetime. Younger generations need what godly seniors have to offer. Likewise, younger generations, who are still in the early spring of their life, have so much to offer seniors in the form of energy and enthusiasm. Like a successful sports team, even the more experienced "pros" can lose their youthful passion for the game without the infectious, reinvigorating enthusiasm of younger, rookie players. Intergenerational friendships and fellowship are a mutually beneficial situation.

Core Value 10
Challenging seniors to reach their spiritual potential

When we speak of challenging someone to "reach their potential," we most likely think of children or teens who may not be applying themselves as much as parents or teachers would like for them to do. When we think of someone reaching his potential, we're probably more inclined to think of the rookie athlete who has the natural talent to go far but still needs a few years of experience on the professional level before hitting his stride. When we think of potential, we usually don't think of seniors. When it comes to reaching our spiritual potential, however, it's a lifelong project. We don't reach our spiritual potential in our youth or even as middle-age adults. In fact, we never ultimately reach our fullest potential. Rather, it's a lifelong process and challenge. This is why, as mentioned in the first chapter, a fundamental difference between the old and a new perspective of seniors ministry is that a new

41

paradigm recognizes that seniors ministry is as much about developing opportunities for seniors to serve as it is about meeting their needs.

Although it may be unintentional, a seniors ministry program that coddles and patronizes more than it challenges and inspires sends a clear message. That message is that seniors have no remaining potential and nothing of value left to offer. When Peter urged believers to "*grow in the grace and knowledge of our Lord Jesus Christ*" (2 Pet. 3:18), he wasn't excluding seniors. When Jesus challenged followers to "*be perfect (i.e. fully grown, complete or mature), even as your heavenly Father is perfect*" (Mt. 5:48), He wasn't just speaking to younger generations. No one ever actually "arrives."

If anyone would seem to have "arrived," surely it would have been the Apostle Paul and yet, even Paul said, "*Not that I have already obtained all this, or have already been made perfect, but I press on to take hold of that for which Christ Jesus took hold of me. Brothers, I do not consider myself yet to have taken hold of it. But one thing I do: Forgetting what is behind and straining toward what is ahead, I press on toward the goal to win the prize for which God has called me heavenward in Christ Jesus*" (Phil. 3:12-17). As if that wasn't convincing enough, listen to what Paul says in the very next verse. "*All of us who are mature should take such a view of things. And if on some point you think differently, that too God will make clear to you.*" In other words, even the mature among us have yet to fully realize their fullest potential.

Core Value 11
Reflecting God's priority for seniors and ministry with seniors

Since the Garden of Eden, God has always expected our best. The reason Cain's sacrifice was inferior to Abel's was not because Cain, as a farmer, offered fruits of the soil to the Lord for his sacrifice while Abel, a keeper of flocks, offered animals. The difference was that whereas Cain merely offered "*some*" of the fruits of the soil, Abel "*brought fat portions from some of the firstborn of his flock*" (Gen. 4). The only way we can authentically honor God, whether in sacrifice or in service, is with a "first-fruits" effort (Prov. 3:9). When David was instructed by God to build a sacrificial alter to the Lord and he had an unexpected opportunity to do so at no cost to himself because of the well-intended generosity of another, David, insisted, "*I will not sacrifice to the Lord my God burnt offerings that cost me nothing*" (2 Sam. 24).

God deserves and expects nothing less than our best. He never expects more than we can do, but He expects our very best. The divine standard for all that we do, whether in word or deed, is "*Whatever you do, work at it with all your heart, as working for the* Lord" (Col. 3:23). We should ask ourselves whether our seniors ministry efforts are better represented by Cain or by Abel. Do our ministry efforts look more like a "Cain" or an "Abel" kind of ministry effort? If seniors ministry is as important to God as the message of this book suggests, then we need to begin making an effort that is more reflective of God's *priority* for seniors and ministry with seniors.

Core Value 12
Equipping and empowering congregations for exceptional ministry with seniors

Seniors ministry needs to be pursued not only on an individual effort basis but also as a *congregational* effort. In fact, it also needs to be approached on a Christendom-wide basis. When it comes to seniors ministry, equipping and empowering others plays as important a role as it does with any other exceptional ministry effort. When Jesus commissioned the apostles, He not only told them to make disciples but to teach them *everything*, which included making disciples. While Paul was mentoring Timothy, he not only trained him to make disciples, he instructed him to teach others so they, in turn, could teach others also. These, in turn, would teach others (2 Tim. 2:2). The very essence of "bearing fruit" implies multiplying ourselves, as well as our efforts. An exceptional seniors ministry program, then, will seek to increase the number of *people* involved in seniors ministry as well as the amount of *efforts* with and for seniors. We have all been given the ministry of reconciliation (2 Cor. 5:18). God's vision for whatever ministry efforts we're making is to include and involve as many others along the way as possible to maximize our efforts.

As a general rule, our seniors ministry efforts are either seriously underdeveloped or virtually non-existent. This is not to say that we are doing "nothing" with seniors. Rather, it simply means that from a well organized, dynamically led, sufficiently funded perspective (think your typically exceptional youth ministry program), a *bare minimal* amount of time, attention, and resources are comparatively given to seniors ministry. Too many of our seniors ministry efforts typically consist of little more than visiting seniors when sick or in the hospital, being more attentive during the loss of a spouse, and perhaps providing some senior a ride to church. Some individuals are also conscientious enough to periodically call just to check on the widows for no apparent reason other than to lovingly check in on them. Some churches have occasional "potlucks" for seniors, send/take them fruit baskets during the holidays, and maybe even schedule an occasional group trip for a social outing. Beyond that, we generally have little more to offer in the way of seniors ministry. These are great and noble beginnings for seniors ministry, but they are only beginnings and they are a far cry from the exceptional effort God's high priority requires.

Compared to our youth ministry endeavors, our ministry efforts with seniors are, at best, rather paltry. Imagine if all we did for youth was provide a ride to church, visit them when hospitalized or when there was a death in their family, give them an occasional call on the phone, periodically mail them a music CD, and occasionally schedule pizza parties and trips to Six Flags. As a general rule, churches are in desperate need of being equipped and empowered for developing a state-of-the-art seniors ministry program, where the ministry needs of seniors are no longer being overlooked and underserved.

CHAPTER THREE
Half Empty Or Half Full?
(obligation or opportunity?)

There is nothing very exciting about obligations. Obligations, like responsibilities, have a negative connotation. They are something we *have* to do more than *get* to do. No doubt, being "responsible" and meeting our "obligations" are mature and noble virtues, but they are rarely considered fun or enjoyable. Obligations are more like doing chores when we're children. Chores are good to have and good to do (from a parent's viewpoint and from a character building perspective), but they're not something we usually look forward to or even remotely enjoy doing. At best, we look forward to getting done with them. Obligations are like bills due at the end of every month. In fact, financial indebtedness is sometimes even referred to as financial "obligations." We may enjoy driving a new car or living in our dream home, but paying that car note or making that mortgage payment every month feels much more like an obligation than it does an opportunity, emotionally speaking.

One of the reasons we aren't as enthusiastic about seniors ministry as we are about other ministry efforts is because ministry with seniors can be misperceived more as an obligation than an opportunity. It may be acknowledged as an honorable or responsible thing to do, but all too often it isn't perceived as an enjoyable and rewarding thing to do. It's human nature to prefer doing things that are enjoyable while avoiding what we perceive would not bring us joy. Until we begin seeing age in a more favorable light, seniors ministry will continue to be perceived more as an obligation than an opportunity.

Fun Meters?
An obligatory perspective of seniors and seniors ministry is a faulty foundation upon which to build an exceptional seniors ministry program. In fact, obligation is as faulty a foundation for ministry efforts as it is for living one's life for God. The value placed on a life for and service to God should not be guided or determined by a "fun" meter any more than the value of seniors ministry should be assessed by a "sensational" meter. Our life for and service to God should be guided and determined by God's priorities – not in some obligatory, legalistic "*have to*" sense, but rather in a shared priorities "*get to*" sense. To illustrate, when something is really, really important to my wife, it naturally and automatically becomes important to me. It

45

becomes important to me whether or not it had been previously and regardless of how much "fun" it may be for me personally. If it's something that weighs heavily upon my wife's heart or gives her great joy, I don't have to be "nagged" or "shamed" into it. It is not perceived as some dreadful obligation to avoid. Rather, that priority actually also becomes my priority because of my love for my wife and my desire to be of one mind, one heart, and one spirit with her.

The same should be true in our relationship with God and His priorities. If seniors are so important to God that He included them in the Ten Commandments (Ex. 20) and uses ministry with them to epitomize the very essence of "pure religion" (Jm. 1), then seniors and seniors ministry becomes important to me. It's important to me because what's important to God becomes important to me. It becomes important to me not out of obligation, but out of love for God and for the pure joy of being one in mind, heart, and spirit with His priorities. To approach life and ministry any other way, whether individually or congregationally, is to care more about our own priorities than God's. To live our life any other way demonstrates the epitome of selfishness and self-centeredness, rather than the essence of godliness and God-centeredness.

Me + Seniors Ministry = Meaningful

Another foundational "crack" in an *obligatory* perspective toward seniors and seniors ministry is that seniors ministry is every bit as personally rewarding and fulfilling as any other important ministry. The choices before us are not "either-or" ... either *enjoy* being an active part of an exciting youth ministry program ... or *endure* being duty bound miserable as an obligatory part of an unfulfilling seniors ministry effort. This is not to say that seniors ministry is for everyone. Youth ministry, children ministry, college ministry, preaching ministry, music ministry, support group ministry, counseling ministry, divorce care ministry, ushers/greeting ministry, inner city ministry, or any other good ministry is not for everybody either. God has gifted each of us differently. That must be respected. However, even if youth ministry isn't your "cup of tea," at least it generally isn't perceived as an obligatory burden. Rather, it's readily recognized as a wonderful opportunity.

The challenge of visualizing seniors ministry as a positive, rather than a negative, experience centers on deciding whom we'll choose to rule our perceptions about seniors ministry – God or a youth-focused culture. In a youth-focused culture youth rules, but in a God-focused culture (which is what the church is *supposed* to be), God rules. So should those priorities that are nearest and dearest to His heart. He and His priorities should rule in our hearts and in our daily lives ... and His priorities should be clearly reflected in the ministry efforts of the church. If seniors ministry is not a high priority of a church's ministry efforts, then that church is neither sharing in one of God's highest priorities, nor are they experiencing a ministry effort that, contrary to common misperception, is an extraordinarily meaningful and personally rewarding opportunity.

Meaningful Moments

Some of the most meaningful moments in my own personal ministry efforts have been with seniors. My experiences as both a teacher and a preacher among people of all ages have been enjoyable. Through the years, all the times I've spent working with teens and college students, as well as with singles, has likewise been gratifying, as has co-directing summer camps for kids and providing pastoral counseling for those in need of encouragement and guidance. I've also experienced deep joy in ministry with *seniors*. For several years now, I have visited senior living facilities in my community on a regular basis providing weekly devotionals for the residents. The experience has been anything but obligatory. On the contrary, those weekly occasions with seniors have been highpoints in my week - highpoints that I look forward to every time. Seniors are some of the most appreciative people to whom I've ever ministered in my life. They are deeply grateful for the special time, attention, and love.

You Are Coming Back Next Week Aren't You?

At the first senior living facility I began visiting regularly years ago, the seniors were so appreciative that even after I had been faithfully coming week after week for several months, they kept expressing concern about whether I'd stop coming. With a tinge of concern in their voice and a trace of worry in their eyes, they would ask at the end of each weekly devotional, *"You are coming back next week, aren't you?"* This would have been understandable after the first two or three weeks – or perhaps even after a month or more. But after nearly half a year of faithfully returning week after week, they would come up to me, time and again, at the end of our time together and ask for reassurance about my return the next week. To be so appreciated and wanted is far from an obligatory experience.

Standing Ovations?

At one senior living facility where I've visited the residents and provided weekly devotionals for years, I've literally been greeted on more than one occasion with a standing ovation just for coming! That's not a commentary on me, as much as it is a commentary on them – the level of appreciation and gratitude they have for someone who cares enough to simply show up regularly to visit and build a relationship with them. They need and appreciate the ministry care that much. I've noticed that most of those "standing O" times have occurred when I had missed visiting with them the previous week due to a rare scheduling conflict. Apparently, it was their spontaneous and subconscious way of expressing just how much those weekly visits mean to them and just how much they didn't want them to stop. Who would have thought that seniors ministry could be so personally gratifying simply because seniors are so appreciative that they could make you feel like a virtual "rock star" for simply caring

47

enough to spend some meaningful time with them on a regular basis. Seniors ministry is a very rewarding experience, not an obligatory one.

Appreciation Out The Wazoo!

Time and again, I've had staff people at the senior living facilities that I regularly visit come up to me as I'm arriving or as I'm leaving to enthusiastically tell me how much they appreciate my weekly visits. This has included executive directors, activities directors, nurses, caregivers, receptionists, and even family members who are visiting. They've been not only appreciative on behalf of the residents, but *personally* appreciative, as they've had occasion to "eavesdrop" on the devotionals and witness the laughter, hugs, prayers, songs, and inspirational messages. On many occasions, they've explained to me how the devotionals are literally the highlight of the week for the residents, more so than any other activity on the calendar of events. It means that much to them because they're that hungry for the special, spiritual attention.

Staff members have also shared with me how much of a blessing it is for them, too, when they've had an opportunity to listen in and observe, while working nearby or passing through to another part of the facility. In fact, one Sunday afternoon an Activities Director told me how she had planned her entire schedule that day (which included updating the nearby wall size bulletin board of activities for the month) so she could listen in on our devotional time, since her work schedule kept her from attending her home church services that morning. Serving in seniors ministry is every bit as personally rewarding and fulfilling as being involved with any other good ministry effort.

This Was JUST What I Needed!

Recently at one of our weekly devotionals at a senior living community, while we were singing hymns before the devotional lesson, the middle-age daughter of a resident came dragging down the hall from apparently having just visited her mother on the health care side of this facility. As she came into range of our singing, her gate slowed even more as she began to look for a place nearby to sit and rest her obviously weary soul. After finding a place to sit, she slumped into a chair, setting down her purse and a big heavy bag which I presumed contained personal items she was toting from her mother's room back to the car. Her face, as well as her body language, spoke unmistakably of just how exhausted she was, both physically and emotionally.

As the devotional progressed from the hymn singing, to the prayer, to the devotional lesson, I couldn't help but occasionally notice her facial expressions throughout the rest of the devotional. There was enthusiastic head nodding in acknowledgement to what was being shared in the lesson along with some occasional smiles. Although I initially wondered if it had been my imagination, the message of her entire body language seemed to transform from that of being tired and exhausted to relaxed and refreshed. She confirmed my suspicion when, after the devotional, she came up to me and said, *"This was just what I needed after the kind of day I've had!"* She then proceeded to thank me profusely for taking the time to come. Then, this previously weary soul went on her way with a smile on her face.

Come Here And Give Me A Hug !

I recall once making my way around the circle at the beginning of one of my devotional visits, hugging all the seniors (who were already all *regular* attendees). On that day, we had a *new* resident to the community who had never attended one of our devotionals until that day. As I approached her, I asked for permission to give her a hug and then stepped back a little as "body language" to give her permission to feel comfortable to decline. This senior politely declined a hug but watched closely as I continued my way around the room, hugging all the other seniors present. At the end of our devotional time together, I again began making my way around the semi-circle of seniors, giving out my hugs and saying my goodbyes. After I finished hugging the senior sitting right next to this new resident, and even while I was still turning toward her to reach out and merely shake her hand, she flashed a big smile, held out her two arms toward me like a little child reaching up to a parent and said with great enthusiasm, *"Come here and give me a hug!"* It thrilled the whole room, as everyone began to chuckle.

On that day, I enjoyed a double victory. Not only did one leery senior experience giving and receiving a much needed hug, the entire room of seniors (including the new resident) burst out in laughter and delight. In fact, you might call that occasion a triple victory because it accomplished even more than blessing a senior in the midst of uncomfortably new surroundings with a needed hug while giving all the other seniors an opportunity to enjoy a hearty laugh. It, perhaps far more significantly, gave every senior in that room (including the new resident) an opportunity to bond with each other over something they were now *all* "in on" together – expressions of holy love for one another.

Maybe Just A Little One

I recall yet another occasion when a resident was hesitant to accept a hug – an occasion that eventually brought healthy laughter to that room full of seniors. Once again, while I was making my way around the room giving out my hugs, there was a new resident in a wheelchair, whom I saw out of the corner of my eye "sizing me up" somewhat skeptically. Since I already knew all the other seniors, all she witnessed was a "stranger" hugging each senior and kissing them on the cheek or forehead, just like I do my own mother. As the only new resident present, she had no idea that I would first stop and ask for her permission, rather than just presumptuously give her a hug and a kiss – so there's no telling what was going on in her mind and heart as I came closer and closer to where she was sitting.

49

When I stood before her, paused, and then asked permission, she eyed me rather suspiciously as she contemplated the situation. You could almost hear the wheels turning in her head as she pondered the "dilemma." While I cordially waited for her reply as to whether I could give her a hug, she gave the most hilarious response that tickled all the other residents. She timidly said, *"Well ... maybe a little one."* This brave soul, in the midst of new surroundings and a room full of unfamiliar faces, boldly took a "risk" (i.e. a step of faith) and gave a complete stranger permission to love her in a holy way. Again, a bonding took place in that almost "magical" moment. I left the devotional that day, as I do every time, feeling privileged, not obligated, to have been there.

You'll Never Know How Much ...

Some of the most joyful and amazing feedback I ever received was from a wheelchair bound resident who had been faithfully attending the weekly devotionals for years. During our singing, she was one of the ones who always sang the most enthusiastically. And every week, while I was giving out my departing hugs, she always whispered a few words of appreciation in my ear about how helpful and encouraging the devotional lesson was for her that day. On this day, however, she had something unusually important to tell me. She gripped my hands just a little more tightly than usual as I was about to give her a hug and a parting kiss on the cheek. She looked straight at me with a message in her eyes that said she had something weighing upon her heart that she simply had to share with me.

On numerous previous occasions, she had briefly reminisced with me about bits and pieces from her past because of something I may have said in the devotional that triggered a memory. On this occasion, however, she said one of the most unexpected things I could have ever imagined coming from the lips of an aging and frail senior. It spoke volumes about the value of ministry with seniors such as this precious but fragile soul, even though she was being cared for in one of the most luxurious senior living communities in our city. In such a sweet, soft voice, and with a hint of sadness, she said, *"I wish you had been my daddy."* This is something you might expect to hear from an inner city child who has never known her father or who had been abandoned at an early age. You might even expect this from some Alzheimer or senility ridden senior who was, in her confused state of mind, drifting back to her childhood days and mistaking you for her actual father. However, for one with a completely lucid mind to make such a statement is both unexpected and seemingly inexplicable unless you had been privileged, as I had been, to share in our periodic little chats at the end of our weekly devotionals when she would take those fleeting moments to share bits and pieces of her heart and life with me.

On a previous occasion she had mentioned to me how her father had died when she was still a child and how she was raised without the benefit of a loving, caring father. Without such previous precious conversations, her statement could have been attributed to senility. However, having already shared from her past, the comment she shared immediately made perfect sense. Near the end of her life, where life was again as fragile and vulnerable as it had been during the childhood years of her fatherless life, she was finally receiving gentle, caring love from someone who reminded her of the father she never had the opportunity as a little girl to know. After all these years, she was finally experiencing the tender, loving, fatherly comfort she still so desperately needed. Seniors ministry truly is a joy, not an obligation.

I'm Going Blind, And I'm Scared!

At the end of one weekly devotional, while I was giving out parting hugs, one senior resident had a look on her face that immediately informed me that she had something very important to share with me. As she grasped my hands tightly, she lowered her voice and whispered, "*I'm going blind, and I'm scared.*" The depth of concern in her eyes spoke volumes. The prospects of living the remainder of her life without sight were all but overwhelming for her to bear alone. The very thought of losing her ability to see family or friends and developing an even greater level of dependence upon others was almost incomprehensible. As I continued to listen, she explained that there was apparently no known treatment to prevent or slow down the process. As we prayed together, I was honored that she felt close enough to open up her heart to me in such a personal way. I was also deeply grateful that God had chosen me to bear this heavy burden with a fellow believer, if only through a hand squeeze, a holy kiss on the cheek, and a prayer. This senior believer needed someone to share her burden. I praise God He chose me to be there for her that day. It just doesn't get any more meaningful and fulfilling than this!

The Misperceptions Of A "Jeh Jeh Jeh" Generation

It is a misperception coming from those "on the outside looking in" that seniors ministry is somehow less rewarding than other ministries. As one on the "inside," I know firsthand that it is a misperception, but I also know why the misperception exists. It comes back to our youth-focused culture. When was the last time you heard an adult longingly say with a sigh, "*I wish I was already old!*"? It not only doesn't happen, it's unfathomable for most. Instead, what is usually said (or at least thought) is how we wish we were *young* again. Our youth-focused culture and perhaps our human nature encourage us to look more favorably upon youth than upon age. Apparently nobody wishes they were old. Teenagers may wish they were old*er*, so they could get their driver's license or purchase adult beverages, but that's just a wish to be old*er*, not old.

The 60's rock group The Who clearly summarized American culture's disdain for age in their song, "My Generation," which includes the lyrics "*I hope I die before I get old.*" Wow! Becoming a senior must really be bad if the "alternative" to life (i.e. death) is preferable to growing old. Years later, another musician, John Cougar Mellencamp, perpetuated similar youth-focused cultural sentiments in his song "Jack and Diane." The song is about the inevitable tragedy of growing up and "losing our youth." The lyrics say, "*Oh yeah, life goes on long after the thrill of living is gone.*" According to the gospel of a youth-focused culture, there is apparently no joy in life once we've grown older. In our youth-focused culture there is a stigma attached to age. Our culture's anthem seductively whispers that youth is good, and age is bad. In fact, age is apparently so bad that we don't want to grow old, even though this is God's divine plan. Growing older is apparently so undesirable that we also prefer avoiding even an indirect affiliation with it (e.g. being associated with seniors ministry) because of the negative connotation we allow to reside within our minds and hearts.

The irony is that this desperate desire to avoid or deny age is about as true among seniors as it is among those who are not seniors – perhaps even more so. Many seniors (especially younger seniors) don't appreciate being identified as "seniors." If you doubt this, try announcing an activity "for seniors" and see how many seniors *don't* show up – not because they're unavailable but because they refuse to be identified with "old folks." The negative image surrounding age creates the presumption that just like *being* old connotes negativity, *ministry* with seniors does, too. In their minds, anything associated with seniors could not possibly represent a positive opportunity or a rewarding experience. The point is, our misperception about age distorts our ability to see seniors ministry as God sees it.

The Joy of Helping Seniors Laugh

Part of the format for our weekly devotionals includes sharing some humor. Years ago, when I first began gathering bits and pieces of humorous and interesting material (jokes, funny stories and interesting background information like Paul Harvey's "The Rest of the Story"), I found myself heavily relying upon many emails that were being forwarded to me from an old college buddy in Texas. Because I was using so much material that came from him, I decided to make the humorous portion of my devotional visits with seniors a bit more colorful by creating a "routine" or "shtick." He became an "invisible sidekick" of sorts. Since much of the material I was using was coming from this Texas friend anyway, I began crediting *all* the humor I used to him. When I began constantly referring to *my ole friend from Texas*," the humor and entertainment offered more than mere humor. The humor, when credited to my "*old friend from Texas*," eventually took on a life of its own by painting pictures in the minds of my senior friends of some fun-loving, mischievous, dusty cowboy hat wearing, ranch owning, scraggly grey bearded, boot wearing ole Texan who loves to spin tall tales. He eventually took on "legendary" status among the seniors whom I visit. Eventually, I began telling stories and sharing the humor as if they were about my Texas friend's own personal life.

For example, if the humor used is about hilarious things children sometimes say (think Art Linkletter's "*Kids Say The Darnedest Things*" from years ago), I'll credit it

52

to something one of my Texas friend's grandchildren said to him the other day. Even if it's just a humorous story about some fictitious character, I'll credit it to actually having happened to "my ole friend from Texas." He has become my "silent partner" for the entertainment portion of the visit. His invisible presence lightens and brightens the day of seniors by providing an additional reason for a few weary souls to have a good laugh. The point is, even with something as seemingly inconsequential as sharing humor, a little ingenuity with a personal touch can spell the difference between mediocre and exceptional ministry with seniors.

"What Do We Hear From Our Ole Friend From Texas?"

One day while I was entering the room to begin giving out my hugs and kisses before our devotional time together, a senior came whirling up to me in his wheelchair enthusiastically asking with the anticipation of a kid on Christmas Eve, *"Well, what do we hear from our ole friend from Texas this week?"* He could barely contain himself to discover what the latest "mess" my friend from Texas might have gotten himself into this week. If you'll re-read this senior's question above, you'll notice that he didn't say "your" ole friend from Texas, but an endearing "our" ole friend from Texas. It's not that any of them actually "believe" the tall tales I share are literally true, anymore than an audience believes a ventriloquist's puppet is "real."

This "shtick" is not intended to mislead or deceive but to merely entertain as well as refresh, and the seniors know it. In fact, a few have been somewhat skeptical that I even have such a friend from Texas – but it only enhances the delight they take in hearing about his weekly mischievousness. From the moment I begin saying, *"You'll never believe what my ole friend from Texas has to share with us this week,"* you can see one senior "roll his eyes" while another silently giggles to herself. Another may "wink" to a friend while yet another gently elbows someone nearby in acknowledgement of the latest "spoof" that they're all about to enjoy. The point is, when you can witness an aging, partially paralyzed, wheelchair bound, world war veteran gleefully wheel up to you with a grin on his face while others begin winking and elbowing each other expectantly just because you've walked into the room, even the biggest skeptic about the joy of seniors ministry can begin to see how seniors ministry is anything but an obligation.

Negative Perceptions Distort Reality

Some of the negative perceptions we have about age is understandable. As the famous entertainer Bette Davis once reportedly quipped in her later years, *"Old age is no place for sissies."* We do experience more limitations as we grow older. We can't move as quickly. We're not as limber as we once were, and we don't feel as good as we did when we were younger. Our endurance is less than before. More aches and pains come with age, and it's not only happening to us. We not only have to personally endure it, we also have to witness it happening to our loved ones, whether a parent, spouse, sibling, or friend. An increasing number of younger seniors are *witnessing* the aging of their own parents, even as they begin personally *experiencing* it themselves!

Depending upon how difficult and how protracted the circumstances, middle-age children of seniors who have gone through or are going through the exhausting challenges of a parent or parents in declining health may, understandably, have difficulty associating anything "positive" with growing old. They may be as unable to see anything positive about seniors ministry as they are incapable of having any favorable feelings associated with growing old. Given such circumstances, it would be inappropriate to even attempt to convince them otherwise. They need and deserve time and space. In fact, they may never be able to personally see or experience the joy of seniors ministry but that's okay.

Seniors ministry isn't for everyone ... and neither is youth ministry or children's ministry or inner city ministry. However, having acknowledged that difficult personal circumstances may disallow some individuals from experiencing the joy that comes with seniors ministry, this does not validate the prevalent cultural misperception that seniors ministry is little more than an unpleasant obligation. Neither should believers allow it to rule their minds and emotions. The personal rewards of ministry with seniors are every bit as meaningful and rewarding as they are with any other ministry. Our misperceptions about age merely distort our ability to see that seniors ministry is not an experience of dismal obligation but one of joyful opportunity.

Every Age Group Has An Obligatory "Burden Factor"

Seniors are no more an obligation than any other age group. Or stated positively, seniors present as much of an opportunity as any other age group – *different* opportunities than those presented by youth, but opportunities that are nevertheless just as valuable and utilizable. Every age group has some degree of a "burden factor," whether from a financial or stress-level perspective. However, that in no way diminishes their value, worth, or potential. Neither should it justify viewing them, whether subconsciously or otherwise, as more of an obligation than an opportunity.

Babies have a "burden factor." Having a child places a burden on the parents from the moment of pregnancy. For some, there is the burden of simply trying to get pregnant. For all new parents, there is the burden of numerous visits to the doctor's office as well as the hospital bill. For some, there is the burden of complications. After birth, there is the burden of diapers, formula, clothes, middle-of-the-night feedings, endless crying, sickness, and accidents. There may be a burden in the form of unpaid medical bills that have to be absorbed and passed on to taxpayers. Still other burdens are babies who become future drug addicts, criminals, and gang members. Such future burdens only place an ever greater strain on law enforcement, our legal system, and already over crowded prison facilities ... if you want to focus *only* on the negative side, as we seem to do with seniors. Pre-adolescents ("tweens") also have a "burden factor." There is an endless list of burdens that arise from having a young child around. They may include babysitter expenses, PTO meetings, transportation to and from sport activities, broken arms, braces, and childhood diseases ... if you want to focus *only* on the negative side, as we seem to do with seniors.

Teens also have a "burden factor." They may include rebellion, bad grades, school fights, loud music, braces, continually out-growing clothes and shoes, eating parents out of house and home, being wasteful, dropping out of school, causing higher car and health insurance premiums, gang associations, doing drugs, and promiscuity ... if you want to focus *only* on the negative side, as we seem to do with seniors. College students aren't exempt from the "burden factor" either. Their burdens may include finding scholarships and grants, taking out loans, experiencing the empty nest, fraternity and sorority parties, hazing, dropping out, flunking out, unemployment, dead-end jobs, unplanned pregnancies, ungodly abortions, and fatal car accidents - if you want to focus *only* on the negative side, as we seem to do with seniors.

Young adults don't escape the "burden factor." Their burdens may include choosing the wrong mate for a spouse, "coming out of the closet," dead-end jobs, borrowing money they'll never re-pay, risky co-signed loans, calling or visiting parents too seldom, moving far away, and moving back home with parents indefinitely - if you want to focus *only* on the negative side, as we seem to do with seniors. Even middle-age adults have a "burden factor." Their burdens may include spousal abuse, child abuse, "workaholicism," medical conditions, affairs, separations, broken homes, divorces, unplanned pregnancies, career crises, and mid-life crises - if you want to focus *only* on the negative side, as we seem to do with seniors.

If Everyone Has A Burden Factor, Then Why Are Seniors Viewed Differently?

The point is, everyone has a "burden factor" – not just seniors. Why, then, are all these other age groups given a "pass" and are still essentially seen more as an opportunity than as some burdensome obligation? Why are seniors and seniors ministry seen (emotionally and subconsciously) more as a burden and an obligation than an opportunity? When every age group has their own share of "burden factors," why do we enthusiastically pursue ministry with others (as often reflected by church budgets and programs), while we treat seniors ministry more as an obligatory afterthought? Seniors can be no more "burdensome" than any other age group – or stated positively, they offer just as much potential opportunity as any other age group. What, then, is the cause of this striking discrepancy and obvious inequity? I can offer no legitimate explanation other than that it always comes back to our youth-focused culture and to how we may be following our own priorities, instead of God's.

If You're Going My Way, I'll Go With You

Sometimes the priorities we pursue, which we *presume* are God's priorities, may actually be our own personal preferences and priorities, which merely happen to coincide with God's priorities. How can this be? Allow me to illustrate with the lyrics of an old song. In the 1970's, there was a song by an artist named Jim Croce called, "I Got A Name," where he's singing about traveling down life's highway and inviting anyone to go with him. The revealing lyrics say, "*If you're going my way, I'll go with you.*" Although it might appear as if this traveler is willing to make the destination of any fellow travelers his priority, too, because he said, "*I'll go with you,*" just the opposite is actually true. The only reason the songwriter says, "*I'll go with you*" is if some fellow traveler just coincidentally happens to be going "*my way*" anyway. That's not really submitting to the fellow traveler's priorities at all. Rather, the two individual's priorities just happen to coincide. In other words, he's still really pursuing his own agenda, not in the least yielding to the agenda of another. On the surface, it could *appear* that the one is honoring the priority of the other, but in reality, he is merely honoring his own, which merely coincides with another's. When we are giving priority to one of God's priorities (youth) to the neglect of another (seniors), we reveal that our high priority pursuits are in actuality our own personal preference and priorities, which just coincidentally align with one of God's priorities.

The "Acid Test"

The "acid test" for whether God's priorities are our priorities is neither demonstrated nor confirmed when a high priority of God's is something we *coincidentally* consider a high priority anyway. Rather, the acid test is when we give high priority to something that we otherwise would not personally assign a high priority status but we do so simply because it's one of God's high priorities and because we long to share in God's priorities. This is not to say that God hasn't given us the freedom to have our own personal priorities from a church ministry perspective. If, for example, having and providing a more "contemporary" worship service is a high priority to a church and its church leaders, God has graciously given us such freedom. But when God has identified specific priorities, they should also become our priorities, not because we *have to*, but because we *get to* and simply *long to* share in God's priorities. If it's near and dear to the heart of God, it should also become near and dear to ours, not out of obligation, but out of privileged opportunity. If it's important to God, we should long to be "*partakers in the divine nature*" of God (2 Pet. 1:4).

As discussed in chapter one, seniors are a high priority to God. They are not an obligation to God but are one of His highly valued priorities which He specifically identifies as such. We need to begin seeing seniors and seniors ministry through the eyes of God instead of through the eyes of *human* wisdom and *personal* priorities, influenced by a youth-focused culture. Through the eyes of God, we would never see

56

seniors ministry as some burdensome obligation but rather would see it as a high priority and delightful opportunity.

CHAPTER FOUR
Where's Webster When We Need Him?
(who is a senior?)

Different Definitions

As surprising as it may sound, a little time and attention should be spent identifying exactly who is a senior. There is no conclusive definition. God hasn't said, although scripture does reveal that God has designed our bodies to last for about 70 - 80 years (Ps. 90:10). Understanding how people, such as Methuselah and others (Gen. 5), lived for hundreds of years nearer the beginning of man's time on earth is for another discussion on another occasion. It is not clear whether this longevity was because something slowly began to change after the fall, something suddenly changed after the flood, or they simply counted time/years differently then than now. Regardless of why, the average life-span is now considerably shorter.

Even in today's world of modern medicine, improved surgical procedures, and healthier living, we are well into our senior years by the time we're in our 70's and 80's. Just as God *has not* clearly defined when one begins becoming a "senior," man *cannot* definitively do so – or at least we apparently can't come to a consensus. According to such organizations as the American Association of Retired Persons (AARP), you apparently become "senior material" when you're 50 years old – at least that's when they begin mailing out invitations for you to become a member. However, for those looking for senior citizen discounts, you're not a "senior citizen" until you're 55. Even the government can't seem to make up its mind about it. Is it 62 or is it 65? Is it 67 or is it 70? There's the PMA (positive mental attitude) crowd who affirms, "*You're only as old as you feel!*" There is the health crowd, who make a distinction between your chronological age and your biological age (the condition of your body). Then, of course, there's the "denial" gang who insist that a senior is "*anyone older than and other than me!*"

It's All A Matter Of Relativity

Admittedly, determining who is "old" and who isn't is somewhat of an exercise in relativity anyway. When I was a child, my elementary school teachers seemed "old," but as someone now in his early 50's, I've come to realize that many elementary school teachers have barely "graduated' from being a teenager. Even someone just in their mid 20's seems "old" to a first grader. As someone still in his early 50's, only the AARP presently considers me a "senior." However, my grandson already teases me about being "old" and "feeble." I think it has something to do with how I run across the backyard more like a wounded water buffalo than a graceful gazelle when we're running "pass patterns" and tossing the football back and forth to each other! It's not that I'm "in denial" about nearly being a senior, as many young seniors seem to be these days. Quite the contrary, I'm what I call an aspiring senior. I look forward to my senior years and intend to embrace and utilize them as fully as possible. I don't look forward to the physical limitations and medical conditions that incrementally (or sometimes suddenly) come with age. I do, however, recognize that the aging process is not some cruel twist of nature but rather is part of God's marvelous plan.

When I was a young boy playing little league baseball in the summer, I thought of my parents as "old," but now I realize they were merely in their 40's. When I was 14 years old, I would have had my driver's license if Texas law had not changed just months before my birthday. At the time, I thought 14 was more than old enough to have a license. Now that I'm in my 50's, the thought of allowing a "child" to drive at 16 (much less at 14) sounds insanely young from today's vantage point. Similarly, when my wife and I married at the age of 19 and 20, how "young" our parents thought we were for marriage seemed irrelevant then. However, the thought of our youngest child, who just turned 20, getting married at his age makes me wonder, *"What were we thinking?"* nearly 35 years ago? When, many years ago, my brother and I planned a 35th wedding anniversary celebration for my parents, I thought anyone who had been married for t-h-i-r-t-y f-i-v-e years was "getting way up there" in years. Now, with my own 35th wedding anniversary knocking on the door, I see it much differently.

A Former Classmate ... Or Former Teacher?

When it comes to our relative perceptions of what "old" is, it reminds me of the story of the man who went to a new dentist for his annual check-up. After being seated in the patient's chair by the assistant and while waiting on the dentist, the patient began pondering whether he may have known the dentist from the past. The patient recognized the dentist's last name, as well as the state where the dentist's diploma on the wall revealed that he had gone to school. As the dentist entered the room, the dentist looked somewhat familiar, but he seemed much too old to be a former high school classmate of the patient. Being curious, however, the patient asked the dentist if perhaps they had known each other from the past. Sure enough, they had been at the same high school during the same time. While the patient was still secretly trying to figure out which classes and teachers they may have both had in school together, the dentist finally confessed that he too had been trying to remember where he had known the patient. He finally asked the patient, *"Were you my math teacher in high school?"* While the patient was trying to decide if the dentist was his

59

former *classmate*, the dentist was trying to decide if the patient was his former *teacher*! The meaning we attribute to age truly is a matter of relativity and personal perspective.

Why It's Important To Identify Who Is A Senior

Simply identifying who is and isn't "senior" is quite relative and therefore relatively meaningless. However, for *ministry* purposes it is a significant question that deserves some serious thought. The reason we should give serious thought to determining who is a senior is because of the age-specific needs and opportunities it presents. Every age group has certain needs unique to that age. Each age group also presents certain unique opportunities. Every age group brings something unique and special to the table. We can either ignore those special needs or identify and minister to them. We can likewise either identify and then utilize the special experience, skills, wisdom, and availability of seniors or squander and lose them.

We understand the value of age-specific ministry when it comes to ministry with younger generations. We understand it so much so that we even identify differing age levels among children. We do this by intentionally sub-dividing them into various age groups to maximize the effectiveness of our efforts. Then, we zealously plan age-specific ministry efforts accordingly, to nurture their needs and cultivate their potential. We wouldn't dream of *routinely* grouping toddlers with teens – or adolescents with adults in a ministry program. We do the same with teens, whom we sometimes sub-divide into younger/junior teens and older teens. We also plan age-specific ministry efforts for college students and young professionals, as well as for singles, divorcees, addicts, the homeless, the unchurched, post moderns and others. It would seem that when it comes to providing exceptional ministry programs for others, we are keenly aware of the value of age or situation specific approaches to ministry.

Then, there are seniors ... and our usually anemic, generic, group-them-with-others, one-size-fits-all ministry efforts. Just as children, teens, and other groups have age-specific *needs* that require age-specific nurturing, so do seniors. Similarly, just like children, teens, and other groups present age and situation specific *opportunities* because of the age-specific and situation-specific ways they can serve in the kingdom, so do seniors. If we intend to provide *exceptional* seniors ministry, we will have to begin more clearly identifying who is a senior. We will also need to begin more proactively identifying their age-specific needs and more fully utilizing their age-specific skills, experience, and availability for service in the kingdom.

We need to develop an age-specific ministry program for seniors. While adults are in their 40's and 50's, there are certain ministry needs they have and certain ways that are more effective in ministering to such adults. However, once adults begin to reach their 50's and 60's, they're coming into an age where their ministry needs are changing again. Those certain ways of ministering to them that had been most effective will eventually no longer be as effective. It's as foolish to continue ministering to young seniors in their 50's and 60's as if they were still adults in their 20's, 30's and 40's as it would be to continue ministering to teens as if they were still children.

In addition to spiritual nurturing, an exceptional ministry program for more seasoned believers will help seniors with preparing for such issues as making a successful transition from career life to the retirement years. It will also provide helpful information about possible options when seniors who have already retired unexpectedly find themselves inadequately prepared. An exceptional ministry program for senior age believers provides leadership, information, and encouragement related to health issues that are of special concern to seniors including such conditions as hearing loss, eye diseases, osteoporosis, prostate problems, impotency, high blood pressure, high cholesterol, and memory loss. Long-term health care is yet another ministry need that seniors will encounter which an exceptional seniors ministry program will address. These and other needs and issues are why, as we begin entering our 50's, 60's, and 70's, churches must make ministry efforts with seniors that are age and situation specific.

Do all middle-age adults develop "senior needs" simply because they've turned 50 or 55 or 62? Of course not, but it's a wise and helpful guideline for exceptional ministry purposes. More importantly, the seniors ministry program should be in place for middle-age adults to move right on into *whenever* the time is right. We should be committed to providing an exceptional seniors ministry program that is so first rate, so impressive, and so appealing that middle-age adults can actually *look forward* to becoming a part of it!

A New Image Can Trump An Old Stigma

Should a seniors ministry program be called a "seniors" ministry program? Arguably and unfortunately, it does present a formidable obstacle because of the stigma that age has been given in a youth-focused culture, and even among God's family of believers. Although this negative stigma is deeply imbedded into the psyche of American culture, this stigma doesn't diminish the ministry needs of seniors. Neither does it lessen the importance of seniors ministry regardless of the terminology used for identifying the ministry effort. The stigma simply needs to be "neutralized" by re-casting the image of being a senior from one with an erroneously negative connotation to a more accurate one with a positive image. Is this "image makeover" an easy task? Can it happen quickly? Will the stigma be completely eradicated? The answer to all three questions is, *"not likely."* The negative stigma associated with seniors can probably no more easily, quickly, or completely be resolved than the erroneous perceptions associated with one race toward another in our culture.

61

There once was (and still is but to a far lesser degree) a need to re-cast the negative image that too many within our culture once had toward people of other races. Similarly, there is a need to do the same about the negative image imposed upon seniors. The erroneously negative connotation that was once more broadly associated with other races of people needed to change. It has been diminished significantly, thanks to the deliberate and intentional efforts of people from all races working together. Similarly, the erroneously negative connotation that is now broadly associated with seniors needs to be re-cast in our culture with the help of young and old alike. If an unjustified and undeserved negative image of racism can and should be changed, it can and should be changed with regards to another "ism" ... ageism. Churches and church leaders have an opportunity as well as a responsibility to help our culture move beyond the "ism" associated with age. Believers young and old alike have both an opportunity and an obligation to help change our culture's perception of what it means to be "senior."

An Image Makeover

When I speak of the need for an image makeover, let me be clear lest I am misunderstood. The kind of image makeover that seniors need is not some vain and foolish attempt to hoodwink others into believing that something that is inherently and intrinsically "bad" is somehow a good thing. This isn't a con job but rather a reality check. Remember the milk commercials years ago? With all the other beverage competition (sodas, beer, juices), someone in the dairy industry finally realized the need for an image makeover and so they developed a campaign that, to this day, has helped cast milk into a more positive and appealing image. The makeover included such slogans as - *"Milk – it does a body good"* and *"Got milk?"* It was accompanied by billboards and television commercials using popular and "cool" celebrities placing their stamp of approval on drinking milk by posing for a publicity photograph wearing a "milk moustache."

The dairy industry finally recognized their image problem and did something about it. Note carefully what they did and did *not* do. They did not represent an inherently and intrinsically "bad" product that required conning or hoodwinking the public in order to market their product more successfully. Rather, they simply yet proactively promoted the positives about their product. Being *"as wise as a serpent, but harmless as a dove,"* they also creatively associated themselves with celebrities to make the campaign not just factually true, but emotionally appealing. That's not deception, but clarification. It's just setting the record straight. Milk isn't a "sissies" drink. It's likewise not just for newborns and "nerds."

Both seniors and seniors ministry likewise need an image makeover. The image of seniors is, generally speaking, a negative one. There are some exceptions, such as grandchildren who may view their doting grandparents in a positive light. However, the most common image of seniors in the mind of a youth-focused culture is one of frail and sickly, cranky and crude, wrinkled and liver-spotted, slow and forgetful, old-fashioned and out-of-touch "old folks" who have already had their turn at life. Such an image is one that is more indicative of people who may actually be valued more for their accumulation of wealth than anything else (think contributions, inheritances, and trust funds).

Where Your Heart Is ...

How we spend our resources, whether as individuals or churches, reveals our high and low priorities in life. Jesus made it abundantly clear that, *"Where your heart is, there will be your treasure also"* (Mt. 6:21). In other words, we'll spend our money on the things that matter most to us. When resources are limited (as they usually are for most), some choose to drive a newer car rather than live in a newer house in a newer neighborhood. They do so because they place more value on cars. Others, however, choose to live in a newer house and a newer neighborhood rather than drive a newer car. They do so because they place more value on their home. Some choose to enjoy life more now rather than plan and save more for the future. Consequently, they set aside less in the form of savings and retirement funds because they place more value on the present. Others, however, choose to plan and save more heavily for the future rather than spend as much in the present.

Churches and church leaders, like individuals, choose how to spend their resources. How they spend their resources is, likewise, a direct reflection of what they value most ... and least. It's an inescapable conclusion, according to Jesus. Some churches choose to have a newer building in a newer location, which leaves fewer resources for other things because they value a newer facility more. Other churches, however, choose to remain in an older building and an older neighborhood, which leaves more resources for other things because they value other things more. On matters where God has not explicitly spoken, He has given churches and church leaders the grace and freedom to establish their own priorities. However, in matters where He has explicitly specified His priorities, we would be wise to make God's priorities our own – and ensure that church budgets and programs reflect it accordingly.

As previously mentioned in chapter one, when a church spends $10,000 per week on youth related programs and $56 per week on seniors ministry, it's a pretty safe bet that such a church and its leaders don't value seniors or seniors ministry very highly. They can deny it all they want, but actions do speak louder than words. How churches allocate ministry expenditures speaks louder than any "lip service" they may pay to seniors.

For example, when a church has multiple ministers on staff (for pulpit, youth, children, worship, and administration, etc.), but not a full-time seniors minister, it's a foregone conclusion that such a church and its leaders don't value seniors or seniors ministry very highly. Such a conclusion is inescapable regardless of how much we may be in denial about it. We typically take a state-of-the-art approach to *youth* ministry while relying on yesterday's solutions for ministry with today's *seniors*. The only way churches and church leaders can *credibly* confirm (not just profess) what they value most is the same way everybody else has to do it: *"Put your money where your mouth is."* They can not just talk a good game. If our ministry efforts and church budgets don't reflect seniors ministry as a high priority, then we are simply at odds with the high value God places on seniors.

Undivided Attention

One of the most important ways the erroneously negative image of seniors and seniors ministry can be re-cast into a positive and more accurate one is by churches having someone give seniors and seniors ministry their *fully focused* attention. This requires having a full-time staff person for the congregation serving specifically and exclusively in that capacity. If part-time or volunteer help was all that is necessary to establish an exceptional seniors ministry program, then one cannot help but wonder why part-time and volunteer help somehow isn't sufficient for providing an exceptional ministry program for *other* ministry efforts that we clearly value so highly. If the need for *exceptional* preaching, teen ministry, children ministry, music and worship, and administration is valued enough to have a full-time staff person working in each of these areas, then why is it so difficult to see that exceptional *seniors* ministry likewise requires someone's fully focused attention?

One Of The Best Kept "Brotherhood Secrets"

In my church heritage, one of our major universities (Abilene Christian University) has a gerontology department. In fact, they've had a gerontology department for many years and have been turning out graduates in that field for quite a while. However, one of the best kept "brotherhood secrets" is that ACU even has a gerontology department. Many, even among those within our church's heritage who consider themselves more informed and on the cutting edge, are shocked to learn this. A few years ago, a gerontology professor there told me that one of the department's most difficult challenges was simply finding a ministry position *in their field* for their gerontology graduates. In other words, despite the fact that a major university has an entire gerontology department – despite the fact that this major university offers a degree in ministry with seniors – despite the fact that this major university proactively promotes their gerontology department through mailings, visits to congregations, and summer workshops for churches – despite all this, ACU's gerontology department is still a resource that is virtually unknown by our churches and church leaders. Again, one must ask why? This same university has a department of which we are fully aware and upon which our brotherhood heavily relies for filling *youth* ministry positions in churches all over the nation.

64

This difference between the ease of placing graduates in their field of youth ministry and the virtual impossibility of placing graduates in their field of seniors ministry likely comes down to one word – *values*. We clearly value youth and youth ministry because youth ministry has a very positive image in the mind of most churches and church leaders. Consequently, we make a point to be fully informed and highly motivated about finding and utilizing the very best of resources for a ministry cause we highly value. The implication is all too clear. We apparently do not value seniors or seniors ministry enough to even know that a prominent university has a gerontology department. We are uninformed because we are disinterested, and we are disinterested, in part, because of the way seniors and seniors ministry have been stigmatized with a negative image.

So, one of the first and most significant things we can do is to have someone fully focused on working with seniors and seniors ministry. Giving seniors ministry someone's full-time attention enables churches to transition more quickly and successfully from having a mediocre seniors ministry program to providing an exceptional one. As more and more mediocre seniors ministry programs become *exceptional* seniors ministry programs, the image of that ministry will change. As the image of seniors ministry changes, exceptional seniors ministry programs will develop in a growing number of churches throughout the land.

Degrading Humor Is Degrading Humor

One of the challenges of identifying seniors for an exceptional seniors ministry program is that seniors dislike being identified as seniors. They dislike being identified as seniors because of the negative image associated with age. One factor that not only perpetuates but propagates this negative image is the use of degrading humor commonly used toward age. This is why an image makeover is so crucial. Churches should take a leading role in countering this negative image by helping restore God's positive image of seniors. One of the easiest but most powerful ways we can accomplish this is to simply discourage degrading humor about growing old. I'm not talking about establishing a spiritual "Gestapo" for ageism that condemns "old jokes" in a legalistic way. Rather I'm simply talking about an intentional effort toward *establishing an atmosphere of restored respect* for age and for seniors by simply recognizing the degrading and destructive nature of depreciating humor (whether about seniors or any other group and whether done by younger generations – or even by seniors themselves). I'm talking about proactively promoting a positive image of age and seniors.

Ageism, in the form of degrading humor, abounds in our culture. Granted, those who are guilty of it may not intend to degrade or de-humanize, but it does so regardless of intentions. How often, after having heard someone make a *racial* slur and when confronted for doing so, has the offender used the excuse "*I didn't mean anything by it*" as their feeble defense? A degrading and de-humanizing racial slur is still a degrading and de-humanizing racial slur. Relying upon such an excuse may merely be the flimsy attempt of a racist to hide his racism. However, it can also be an indicator that such an individual simply isn't aware that he has made a racial remark. Similarly, one who speaks degradingly against those who are older, whether he realizes it or not and even in the name of humor, is likewise guilty of ageism. Unfortunately, being an "ageist" in our culture just doesn't have the same shame factor as does being a racist.

Being racist has finally become widely accepted as ... unacceptable - thanks to the efforts and sacrifice of many. Similarly, until intentional sacrificial effort is made to make ageism as unacceptable as racism, seniors will continue to be unwittingly treated as second class citizens even within their own communities of faith. Is this to say that jokes about age are paramount to uttering the "N" word? Perhaps it is, but not necessarily. I'm not prepared to declare that someone bringing "black balloons" to a friend as a gag on their 30th or 50th birthday party is guilty of "ageism." It does, however, illustrate the negative connotation associated with growing older or becoming senior. I'm not prepared to declare all humorous references to having "senior moments" of forgetfulness as some spiritual crime, but it does illustrate the negative connotation associated with being senior in a youth-focused culture.

My intention is not to place ageism on the exact same level as racism, although there are striking similarities. It's not that we should attempt to "legislate morality" as much as it is that we should be encouraging, inspiring, and restoring respect for seniors. We don't need Congress to pass a law against making good natured fun of milk, and neither is there necessarily anything "wrong" with finding something humorous about milk drinkers. But just like the Dairy Association didn't need Congress to pass a law making it illegal to make fun of milk, we don't need to declare war against poking fun at growing/being old. Just like the Dairy Association simply promoted the positive aspects of milk, the benefits of growing older need to be similarly emphasized by intentionally and proactively promoting the positive aspects of being senior. Degrading jokes about seniors shouldn't have to be argued from a perspective of right or wrong. They should simply be personally offensive – as offensive as a racial slur. In God's world, everyone should be an aspiring senior because that's the way God, the "Ultimate Senior," has planned it.

CHAPTER FIVE
Stop Shooting Yourself In The Foot!
(*what seniors can stop doing*)

Sometimes in life, we can be our own worst enemy. Sometimes, the enemy from without is not nearly as dangerous and destructive as the enemy within. Of all the ideas, suggestions, game plans, and strategies that could be devised, perhaps the single most important and decisive action that could be taken to help advance the cause of exceptional seniors ministry is for seniors to stop "*shooting themselves in the foot.*" They do a grave disservice to themselves as well as to the cause of exceptional seniors ministry by not rejecting such a negative image about age which subtly undermines the worth of seniors. This destructive form of negativity happens on a daily basis. It happens when seniors fall for or at least resign themselves to the inferior status relegated to them by the steady drumbeat message of a youth-focused culture. In a nutshell, that message about seniors is a negative one that says growing older and being older is not a good thing and is inferior to being younger. The message suggests that once you're a senior you've somehow lost value and are less significant. That message says it's time for you to "retire," which is thinly veiled code language for "*get out of the way.*"

In recent years, a few have even gone so far as to begin suggesting that it is a senior's "duty to die" once they reach a certain age. Sadly, this isn't a novice idea, though proponents are becoming bolder. As far back as 1976, a "B grade" sci-fi movie, *Logan's Run*, was about a future where society had determined that everyone over thirty had a duty to die and to be terminated. "Runners" like Logan, who refused to comply and tried to escape sentence, were simply "assisted." If you think espousing such a notion simply because of one's age is limited to Hollywood's fanciful and futuristic sci-fi movies, you'd be "dead wrong."

The former Governor of Colorado, Richard Lamb, once reportedly made a rather shocking statement, bluntly suggesting that seniors had a duty to die and get out of way. More specifically, he said that seniors should, "*Consider making room in the world for the young by simply doing with less medical care and letting themselves die.*" A medical ethicist in a Hasting Center Report (a journal of medical ethics!) said that *"health care should be withheld even for those who want to live"* if they have lived beyond the politically correct number of years (which he suggested might be 75). Other medical ethicists agreed, but "generously" suggested extending the limit to age 80. A brief search of the phrase "duty to die" on the internet will actually bring up a plethora of information on the subject. This "duty to die" mentality is inevitable in a youth-focused society, where seniors are simply seen as an inconvenient *"demographic, economic and medical avalanche"* of problems.

If God's high priority for seniors in a youth-focused culture is ever to be taken seriously, it will most likely be because seniors stop allowing such a culture to dictate the "rules" for life. They will start standing up for themselves which is actually standing up for God's high priority for seniors. But therein is the tricky part. By their very nature, godly seniors are disinclined to stand up for themselves. That is why it's so important for seniors to realize that standing up for seniors is not selfishly standing up for self. Rather, it's selfLESSly standing up for others (for seniors collectively) as well as for God! It's not a selfish but a godly thing to do.

Embrace Our Senior Years

So what can seniors do to help stop all this "foot shooting"? What, exactly, can and should they begin doing? The first thing seniors can do is simply embrace their senior years. It doesn't take being a senior to discover that life isn't quite everything it's cracked up to be. We live in a fallen world, and this becomes apparent long before the later years of life. Wars, accidents, bad choices, and circumstances beyond our control leave everyone with less than an "ideal" life. Even innocent newborns sometimes enter this world with various defects and debilitating handicaps or disadvantaged family circumstances. There is no stage in life where everything is "perfect." Every stage has its advantages and disadvantages. Human nature tempts us to believe the grass is always greener elsewhere than where we presently are – so much so that even difficult times of the past are often granted "good ole days" status, even if they weren't all that great.

Our senior years, admittedly, can present some pretty difficult challenges. However, how we view our life – and more importantly, how we *live* our life, for the most part, is a choice regardless of our age. We must choose whether or not to make the most of our life at *every* stage of life. Whether we're younger or older, we must "play the cards we're dealt" to the best of our ability. This is all God ever expects of us, regardless of age. In fact, it's how we honor Him most.

Our youth-focused culture sends an endless message that growing older is a terrible thing and must be avoided or at least delayed as much and as long as possible. Clever marketing encourages us to "defy" the aging process by using products even though the best these "age defying" products can really do is simply conceal it momentarily. It would be silly to deny that youth has its advantages, but youth has some profound and distinct disadvantages too – hurtful foolishness, insatiable restlessness, and reckless shortsightedness just to name a few. Yes, youth has its advantages, but so does age, for the godly senior. Experience, wisdom, and reliability represent some of the more significant ones. It comes down to this. There are advantages and disadvantages to *every* stage of life. Becoming senior is not better or worse than being young. It's just the next stage of God's marvelous plan, so the only godly thing to do (what God intends for us to do) is embrace our senior years.

The "Young Senior" Challenge

Embracing our senior years can be especially tricky for younger seniors who must decide whether to live either in denial or undeterred by their fading youth. The senior years of our life have less to do with the number of candles on a cake or even our physique and more to do with the depth of our relationship with God. Those who are becoming "young seniors" must decide whether to spend time foolishly in denial that they are now seniors or to live their life undeterred by a cultural attitude about aging. The more that younger seniors live in denial, the more they shoot themselves (and fellow seniors who are even older) in the foot.

Reject The Negative Image

Another thing seniors must do is resist ... no, *reject* the negative image our youth-focused culture tries to impose upon seniors, as has been alluded to previously. Quite possibly, the single greatest disservice our culture has done to today's seniors is "selling" the notion that growing older is an inherently bad thing. This notion not only pervades the American mindset of younger generations, but it has also especially victimized the thinking of both younger and older seniors as well. Churches and church leaders have, likewise, been hoodwinked. Perhaps for the godless, age may well be the ultimate negative, but for the godly senior, age is not just "*better than the alternative*" (i.e. death) – it's a beautiful thing! This thing we call life on earth is not about perpetuating youth, but rather progressing (yes, progressing!) beyond the limitations of youth. Let me repeat that for sake of emphasis. Our time on earth is not about perpetuating youth but rather progressing beyond the limitations of youth. Youth, at best, is fleeting and offers more illusion than the genuine substance and authentic reality that God ultimately intends for us. The godly senior is simply closer to actualizing God's eternal intentions.

Stay In The Game

Seniors, whether younger or older, must also resolve to stay in the game. Our culture would have seniors accept the foregone conclusion that seniors are expected to eventually retire. God, however, has something else in mind, commissioning seniors to remain active and productive even as they grow older and continue being full of inner life and beautiful (Ps. 92:14). Some of the most active and productive people in the Bible who were used the mostly mightily by God were advanced in age. Abraham, Moses, and Noah are some of the more well known examples. While

69

today's churches with little vision for seniors ministry prefer to provide seniors with little more than seasonal gifts, occasional potlucks, and periodic social outings, even the business world is beginning to recognize that times have changed. Today's seniors are more able, willing, and ready to remain purposefully active and meaningfully useful. As so vividly illustrated by the actor Dennis Hopper in TV commercials for a financial investment company, continuing to impose our culture's traditional definitions of "retirement" (*to withdraw, go away, disappear*) is both an outdated and visionless perspective of today's seniors.

Lead The Way
Seniors must also lead the way! Just as the children of Israel needed deliverance from Egyptian slavery, today's seniors need deliverance from the bondage of ageism that pervades not only our culture but even God's family. If today's younger seniors don't lead the way NOW for helping churches and church leaders to begin re-thinking the importance of seniors ministry, these young seniors will not only perpetuate the neglect of today's older seniors, they will eventually and inevitably become victims of their own neglect once they themselves have become older seniors

Beginnings And Endings or Endings and Beginnings?
Another thing seniors can do to stop "*shooting themselves in the foot*" is to reverse their attitude about beginnings and endings. At the beginning of every calendar year, we seem more mindful of new beginnings and fresh starts. For many, the beginning of a new year is a time for putting the past behind and looking forward with renewed intentions and hopes. What better way for seniors to view life at *all* times of the year than from a perspective of new beginnings!

Perhaps God was on to something when He opened the Bible with "*In the beginning.*" Perhaps it's more than coincidentally "backwards" to our culture's way of thinking when, during creation, God spoke of "*an evening and a morning*" … instead of a morning and an evening. Perhaps from the "get go," God was establishing a perspective, as well as setting a precedent, for an entire outlook on life. Perhaps … just perhaps we need to completely re-think our perspective on beginnings and endings, especially when it comes to aging.

Except for the time surrounding every January first, we're conditioned to think more in terms of beginnings with endings than we are endings with new beginnings - whether the beginning and end of a day, a month, a year, a decade, or even a century. We tend to think of life in terms of birth … then death. We think of education in terms of kindergarten … then graduation. We think of books and movies in terms of a start … and then a finish. We tend to think of television shows in terms of a "pilot" beginning and then a season or a series "finale." Even promising, new relationships eventually have their inevitable endings, if only in death. Consequently, except for this one time of the year (January first), we seem more accustomed to thinking in

70

terms of beginnings with endings than we are accustomed to thinking of endings with new beginnings. We need to begin thinking more in terms of *beginnings* than endings, especially when it comes to aging.

Life is not nearing an *end* as we transition into our senior years, but rather it is nearing the *beginning*! Our senior years can represent many new beginnings ... for those who choose to see life through the eyes of beginnings more than endings. Our senior years are a time to *begin* to more fully and effectively use the knowledge, skills, and wisdom that we have accumulated by the grace of God after a lifetime of experience. It's a time to *begin* modeling authentic spiritual maturity for younger generations that inspires and is worthy of emulation. Our retirement years are a time to *begin* turning past success into present significance. Ultimately, it will become the time that we'll *begin* spending eternity with God in heaven. Becoming and being a senior is far more about beginnings than it is endings for those who love the Lord and live their life according to His purpose. All too often, however, our thoughts and feelings about growing older betray that even among believers, our aging faith may sometimes be much more grounded in textbook "theory" than in our own personal spiritual reality. When becoming or being a senior has us looking backwards remorsefully more than forward with anticipation, perhaps it's time to re-think endings and beginnings.

The sooner we realize ... or rather *internalize* that becoming or being a senior is not about endings, but beginnings – the better! It's the beginning of retiring "to" rather than "from." It's about discovering and pursuing new opportunities daily that God gives to each of His children, regardless of age - whether children, teens, young adults, middle-age adults, or seniors. It's about discovering new ways and new places in our life to live purposeful, meaningful lives. It's about fixing our eyes more upon the future than the past. It's about a choice we must make *every* day as to whether our perspective during the senior years of our life says, "And in conclusion" ... or "In the beginning!"

Wake Up! Stand Up! Speak Up!

One more thing seniors can do to stop "*shooting themselves in the foot*" is to speak up! Embracing our senior years, rejecting the negative image, staying in the game, leading the way, and reversing our attitude about age lay the necessary foundation for taking action. Attitude without action, however, is meaningless. It's time for the "sleeping giant" of seniors to wake up, stand up, and speak up about God's high priority for seniors and seniors ministry. Several years ago, a senior made the following comment on a feedback form: "*Finally some recognition that not all church activities and ministries should be for young people!*" These were the words a senior said with both enthusiasm and exasperation while attending one of our half-day workshops on seniors ministry. Clearly, the workshop hit a nerve.

Such a statement, even at face value, speaks volumes about the unspoken yearning within this older believer for *exceptional* ministry rather than mediocre ministry with today's seniors. However, what is far more insightful about this senior's statement is what was *not* said or rather *when* it was said. It wasn't said until ... *"finally!"* She didn't acknowledge her true feelings until after having remained painfully silent for far too long. Such disinclination to speak up makes one wonder how many others does this senior's sentiments represent who have not yet "finally" spoken up?

How can an entire generation of believers find themselves so far outside the time, attention, and resources of today's church budget and program priorities – especially when those very churches "stand on the shoulders" of the ones who laid the foundation upon which the existence of those very churches rests? When did it reach a point where substantial amounts of time, attention, and resources are dedicated to *other* ministry efforts, while such limited resources are committed to seniors? Why is it that other ministry efforts can be pursued with such creativity, innovation, and energy while ministry efforts with seniors can be so unimaginative, uninspiring, and outdated?

Perhaps more significantly than how is *what* ... what can be done to encourage *exceptional* seniors ministry? What must be done is for seniors and those who care about seniors to "finally" become vocal about the need for churches to take such a ministry far more seriously and to make seniors ministry a high priority. Although a large part of what defines most godly seniors is their unimposing demeanor, seniors ministry (i.e. God's high priority for seniors) will only become a priority when enough seniors and those who care about seniors stop being silent and "finally" begin lovingly demanding it. They must "demand it" not in some self-centered, narcissistic way, but rather ardently on behalf of an entire generation of believers being left behind in a youth-focused culture.

Until seniors wake up, stand up, and speak up, the ministry needs of today's seniors will probably never receive the time, attention, and resources that God's high priority for them deserve and require. Otherwise, the amount of time, attention, and resources given by churches and church leaders to seniors and seniors ministry will most likely be determined by flawed, conventional wisdom and limited anecdotal evidence. Until the ministry needs of seniors are determined *reliably* by God's priorities instead of unreliably by youth-focused preferences and priorities, churches and church leaders may never begin offering a *substantial* response to the ministry needs of today's seniors.

The challenges, difficulties, and problems of life don't simply disappear with age - they only change. The needs of the spirit and the soul for personal, intentional, and consistent encouragement from the body of Christ don't simply vanish as we grow older. Rather, they become less important to younger generations. An insufficient understanding of the ministry needs of today's seniors results in an insufficient response which only perpetuates neglect. Seniors ministry is such a low priority because we are too unaware of the high priority God has placed on seniors. One primary reason for this low level of awareness is that seniors keep undermining their own cause in ways described in this chapter. If God's priority for seniors is ever to be taken seriously and genuinely honored, it will only begin happening in a significant way when seniors stop *"shooting themselves in the foot."*

CHAPTER SIX
A Session With The Shrink
(assessing needs and giftedness)

Fundamental Needs Of Today's Seniors

Early on, whether merely beginning or seriously expanding seniors ministry efforts in your home church, an assessment of both the needs and giftedness of seniors will be essential. Just as a doctor must not presume anything but must first diagnose the situation to most effectively address the patient's need, we too should not presume anything. Rather, we should first "diagnose" the ministry needs of seniors. The sooner the doctor can accurately pinpoint "where it hurts" (whether by careful observation, examination, or simply asking – or a combination of the three), the sooner the doctor can begin addressing the patient's needs in the most efficient and effective way. Likewise, the sooner we can accurately pinpoint the ministry needs of seniors, the sooner and better their ministry needs will be more effectively and sufficiently met.

Pinpointing the ministry needs of today's seniors requires gaining a better understanding of their needs but this requires *broadening our understanding* of what they are and how best to address them. Trying to identify and address the ministry needs of today's seniors in essentially the same narrow way it was being done 50 years ago is simply inadequate and unacceptable. How effective would a doctor be today if he used the same medical knowledge – the same surgical techniques and procedures – the same medical equipment – and the same medicines as were used 50 years ago? No doubt he could still do some good, but what patient in his right mind would consider such a doctor "up to spec" and acceptable? What doctor in his right mind would consider himself acceptable? What professional medical board would consider it acceptable?

Similarly, how effective would a church or youth minister be with today's teens, if they used the same ideas, methods and techniques used 50 years ago? Some good could still be accomplished, but what teen would be compelled to participate? What churches or youth ministers in their right minds would consider it acceptable? The

74

same is no less true when it comes to ministry with today's seniors. Seniors are people, too! They have ministry needs just like any other age group.

Just as a *needs* assessment is crucial in determining the ministry needs of seniors, a skills or *giftedness* assessment is equally crucial in determining *service* opportunities for how seniors can be most useful and where they are authentically needed. I prefer to use the term "giftedness" over "skills" because giftedness would seem to do a better job of conveying the "God factor" in the ability. Perhaps some might consider this merely a semantic play on words, but the distinction is both valid and significant. This is especially true when it comes to churches and church leaders finding and providing places of meaningful service where seniors are authentically needed.

A Double Opportunity

Just as it is a misperception to think of seniors ministry as an "obligation," it is likewise a mistake to see seniors ministry as anything other than an incredible *opportunity* to be captured and harnessed – from two perspectives. From a church resource perspective, seniors are quite possibly the most overlooked, de-valued, and underutilized resource available to churches today, in terms of "manpower" and availability. From an individual perspective, the "retirement" years of seniors could be their most productive and useful days for the kingdom if they choose to make them so and especially if churches and church leaders begin to encourage, empower, and enable them to do so.

Overlooked And Undervalued

The reason seniors are often overlooked and undervalued is that any serious attempt to carefully and comprehensively identify their skills and experience has too seldom been made. Too little effort has been made to empower them for how best and where to apply their skills and experience for the cause of the kingdom. Consequently, little effort has been made to empower them for where and how they can best apply their experienced skills to ministry opportunities in the kingdom. All too often, attempts to identify and apply the skills and experience of seniors remain limited and superficial. We would be wise to encourage and provide two major assessments for all members … and especially for seniors. One would be for assessing their *needs* and another for assessing their *giftedness*. It will be in the matching of the giftedness of one individual with the need of another individual that the needs will be most exceptionally *met*, while at the same time the giftedness of another will be most exceptionally *utilized*.

Staggering Potential

As previously mentioned in chapter one, seniors represent an increasingly substantial portion of our country's population as well as a staggering potential as a resource for churches and church leaders. Some congregations may consist of primarily younger members because those churches have been intentionally "grown"

75

that way by leaders because of their self-chosen priorities. There are other congregations that may consist of primarily older members because, out of complacency, they've allowed themselves to slowly become that way. On average, about 33% of all Americans and about 50% of all Protestant believers are seniors.

Would Seniors Really Be Missed?

It might sound rather harsh to question whether the primary value we may see in seniors is merely their money, but what significant impact would it really have on most churches if all their seniors were to suddenly disappear? A church's attendance would drop somewhat depending on how many members were seniors, but that's merely a mathematical number. A few older leaders would be gone, but most churches are led by middle-age, successful businessmen anyway. Where the void would probably be most noticeable would be in the pocketbook.

This is not to say that the majority of a church's donations come from seniors. That may be true in some churches and not true in others. It's simply to say that, judging from the minimal amount of time, attention, and resources devoted to seniors and seniors ministry, the primary "value" placed upon seniors by churches and church leaders would seemingly be their money – especially their special contributions, wills, and trust funds. As harsh as this may sound, how else can we explain the glaring inequity between the substantial amount of time, attention, and resources spent on youth ministry programs and the substantially lesser amount devoted to ministry with seniors?

In a world where, according to Jesus, *"the harvest is plentiful, but the laborers are few"* (Mt. 9:37), you'd think that churches and church leaders would be stumbling all over themselves to seriously access and better use this vast resource of potential laborers for kingdom causes. You'd think they'd all be scrambling to establish state-of-the-art seniors ministry programs … if for no other reason than for helping equip, empower, and encourage all these seniors for service in the kingdom. However, we seem to be anything but stumbling all over ourselves. We should do some soul searching to ask ourselves why. Although many seniors are remaining in the "workforce" longer and some retire only to re-enter the workforce, the fact remains that seniors, as a rule, are more "available" than younger generations, who still have their hands full establishing their careers and raising their families.

In addition to seniors being generally more available for service, they also have numerous "crossover" skills and experience to offer that can be applied to various ministry needs and efforts. Whereas we readily see the need to help younger generations "reach their potential," there seems to be no similar ability in readily seeing the need to help seniors reach theirs. Seniors have no more reached their spiritual potential than have our youth. Striving toward "perfection" (Heb. 6:1; 2 Cor. 13:11, 2 Tim. 3:17; etc.) is a lifelong goal that doesn't end simply because we've become seniors. The sooner we focus on the potential of *seniors*, the sooner we will begin accessing and utilizing this vast but largely untapped resource that is right there before us.

Formal vs. Relational Assessments

We will never be in a good position to address the unmet ministry needs of seniors exceptionally unless we begin proactively gaining a broader, deeper, more personal understanding of those needs. We must become more intentional and proactive in our efforts. A *needs assessment* is a helpful tool. This can be done either *formally* or *relationally*. A *formal* assessment is something similar to a *survey* of ministry needs, beginning with senior members of the congregation and then branching out to their senior friends and neighbors as well as other seniors in the community.

A *relational* assessment may seem less efficient (i.e. takes more time and effort than a quick check-list) but is far less impersonal and much more insightful – because it requires building a relationship with those seniors. How reasonable is it for us to expect someone to disclose their innermost feelings about their needs in a superficial survey to someone they may not even know very well anyway? Even if seniors were comfortable enough to share their ministry needs in a survey, the survey's check-list would almost assuredly miss some of their most important ministry needs. Consequently, it isn't likely to provide nearly as much insight as would a relational assessment survey. Let me illustrate.

An Example Of The Value Of Assessing Needs Relationally

Three or four times a year I visit my mother, who lives in another state. When possible, I usually stay for a week at a time. Before I arrive, I encourage her to make a list of things she needs me to do around the house while I'm there. It could consist of things as simple as changing a light bulb in the kitchen or resetting the time and date on her digital answering machine because the electricity momentarily went out weeks ago. It could be something a little more involved, such as re-staining the porch deck or repairing an aging privacy fence. It might entail something a little more complex, such as helping her review and re-evaluate some aspect of an insurance policy or helping her prepare for a devotional lesson she plans to share with the ladies' Bible class or at one of the senior living facilities she visits regularly.

I've learned to encourage her to begin that "to-do" list weeks in advance of my arrival because she doesn't automatically or readily think of everything that she needs to have done – even things that she would consider urgent or important. Like many seniors, she is not a "self" focused individual, so she doesn't obsess over her own wants and needs. In fact, she hesitates to make the list at all, so I always have to encourage her to do it. She wants to be as independent and unimposing as possible. Openly "conceding" that she has an occasional need for help doesn't come naturally for her – even with the advantage of a close mother-son relationship. Imagine how

77

much more difficult or uncomfortable it may be for seniors to concede their needs (i.e. their dependency) when that concession is made to a non-family member in some superficial, check-off, survey list. Once I'm at my mother's house, after having given her weeks of time to incrementally add additional items here and there to the "to do list" prior to my arrival, we still invariably end up adding numerous other items to it. Some items eventually added to the list are needs she remembers only as the week unfolds while I'm there. Others are things I personally observe that need attention. As I call these additional items to her attention, she often says, *"Oh, I intended to include that on the list."*

The point is, although a formal survey would undoubtedly result in a partial list of my mother's needs, there is no way I would receive as insightful an understanding of her needs as I would with a more relational approach. In the course of our week together, as we enjoy conversations and simply spend time with one another, I gain the best and fullest insight to her needs. The most effective way to gain the best grasp of a senior's needs is through a "relational" needs assessment. This, however, takes time as well as effort. It requires actually building a personal relationship with seniors which is how any exceptional ministry effort is best done. Those engaging in seniors ministry don't need to "minister to" seniors as much as they need to build relationships with them. By building a relationship with them, their ministry needs will become more readily apparent and can then be more naturally and effectively met. A relational needs assessment is, by far, the best way to determine the ministry needs of seniors.

Check It Off vs. Check It Out

A *giftedness* assessment can also be accomplished in more than one way. Just as there are inferior and superior ways to assess a senior's *needs* (formal vs. relational), there are inferior and superior ways to assess a senior's *giftedness*. An inferior way to help seniors assess how God has gifted them for service is by using an old fashioned "talent survey," where participants simply work from a check-list of options of how they would like to serve. Depending on that church's cultural heritage of traditions and customs, opportunities to serve from a survey check-list would typically include anything from teaching a Bible class, to leading a public prayer, to serving communion, to being a greeter or an usher - and so forth.

A much more thorough, effective, and reaffirming way to help seniors discover how best they can serve and where they are most needed is through an in-depth, personal, exploratory, "check-it-out" giftedness assessment covering how God has gifted them to serve. One excellent way to do this is with a teacher-guided assessment class in a group setting over a period of several weeks. This might be accomplished on Sunday mornings as a special Bible class series. In such a setting, participants not only have the advantage of group dynamics but also ample time for introspective reflection and thoughtful processing.

Giftedness Assessment Classes

There are numerous materials available for accomplishing such an assessment. Each has their own advantages and disadvantages. As part of the services we provide for sponsoring churches, Sage Ministries offers a teacher-facilitated course on "Discovering My Giftedness." The course is beneficial for people of *all* ages, not just seniors. Since the issue of how God has gifted individuals is not an age-specific topic (i.e. God has gifted everyone – 1 Cor. 7:7; 1 Pet. 4:10; Rom. 12:26; Eph. 4:16), the class can be a mixture of seniors as well as middle-age adults, young adult, and even teens. It could be equally advantageous having an assessment class consisting of seniors exclusively or having one that represented a multigenerational mix. If the class consisted of only seniors, then some seniors might feel more comfortable among their peers and less out of place in a class among those much younger than seniors. On the other hand, if the class consisted of a mixture of all ages, then some seniors might feel a little more comfortable being in a class that isn't just for "old folks."

Either way, you may face some challenges when promoting and encouraging senior involvement for such a class. If, for example, a promotional push is made about a class for all ages on discovering their giftedness, it is quite possible that seniors may not see any need for older believers to attend such a class. Likewise, if a promotional push is made about such a class designated as especially for seniors, seniors may not attend because they'd prefer not to be associated with "old folks." This two-sided dilemma just illustrates how age-specific ministry efforts, though a blessing in many ways, can work to the *disadvantage* of seniors. It can become disadvantageous when age-specific ministry is over-practiced to the neglect of intergenerational ministry efforts. If we aren't careful, the blessing of specialization can become the curse of specializationism.

Capabilities vs. Giftedness

In order for seniors to not only *feel* but authentically *be* needed for meaningful service, they must first know how God has gifted them to serve. If they don't know or are unsure, they need to discover their giftedness from God. Even for those who may *think* they know how God has gifted them for service in the kingdom, many discover that they have spent much of their life nobly serving in areas other than where God has most gifted them to serve. For those who genuinely know how God has gifted them, it is still a very re-affirming experience to attend a "Discovering My Giftedness" class, as mentioned earlier. However, one of the bigger revelations in my life was when I began to realize just how much even people who have been Bible-taught, church-attending, service-oriented, raised-in-the-church believers can still be clueless about how God has gifted them for service in the kingdom. This is not to say that such believers have not been serving, but they may not have been serving in the area in which they are most gifted.

After experiencing a giftedness assessment, many discover that they've been playing into their *capabilities* more than their *giftedness* or even into their *weaknesses* instead of playing into their *strengths* (i.e. their giftedness). From a ministry perspective, there's a big difference between capabilities and giftedness. An athletic individual may have the *capability* to play basketball ... maybe even very *good* basketball, but someone like Michael Jordon was *gifted* for the sport of basketball. He tried playing professional baseball and had the *capability*, but wasn't *gifted* for baseball like he was gifted for basketball. Many believers spend their life in service to God like Michael Jordan playing baseball. They focus on their capabilities when they should be doing what they were *gifted* to do. They may have the *capability* to serve in one area (because of natural ability, education or previous experience), but this doesn't necessarily mean they have been *gifted* by God to serve in that area.

A Backwards Approach

How and why do we find ourselves in a situation where believers may be serving more out of *capability* than out of *giftedness*? When it comes to paid "staff" positions, we usually go about it quite differently. We carefully screen, interview, and even "try out" the staff person, especially if it's the pulpit preaching or youth ministry position, to ensure the individual is "qualified" for the task. However, when it comes to tasks performed by unpaid volunteers, we're not only all too willing to lower the standards for those who fill those positions, but we also seem to turn the process upside down. As churches and church leaders have enlisted volunteers, they've often gone about it "backward" from the way God intended it.

In chapters 12, 13 and 14 of the Apostle Paul's first epistle to the Corinthians, Paul spoke of how the Spirit enabled believers to serve in various miraculous ways. I reference this text not to discuss or debate whether miraculous gifts still exist today but rather to establish God's principle of how believers serve according to the way God has gifted them. When it came to how a believer was to serve (i.e. his place of service in the kingdom), the beginning point was not the need that should be addressed but rather the gift that the believer had been given to offer. In Corinth, for example, the disciples didn't simply see the need for teaching and then begin randomly asking for any volunteers among those who may have been local school teachers who were willing or could be "arm-twisted" into performing that task for the church, regardless of how they had been *gifted* by God to serve in the kingdom. Instead, those who had been given the gift of teaching by the Spirit were the ones who did the teaching. In principle, that's how God originally planned and intended it.

Filling Empty Positions or Exercising Giftedness?

What all too often happens now is that when there is a volunteer task that needs doing or a volunteer position that needs filling, we focus more on simply finding a volunteer who is *willing* to do the task and *capable* of filling the position with too little regard for how, what, and where that volunteer has actually been *gifted* by God

80

for service. As long as he has the *capability*, we're just so relieved and grateful to simply fill the empty position. There is nothing "wrong" with serving in an area where we may have the *capability* but not the *giftedness*. In fact, it's necessary at times. There are always routine and mundane tasks (or even ministry responsibilities) that must be done among any group of believers.

On an individual family level, this may include taking out the trash, walking the dog, or washing the dishes. These are group responsibilities that just need to be done by someone. Anyone who has the capability should help. You don't have to be gifted or to have a calling from God for everything you do. A toddler, for example, may not have the capability to take out the trash, whereas a teenager would ... and should, irrespective of how God may have gifted him for service.

Church family members, like individual family members, also have numerous group responsibilities for which anyone in the group should feel obliged to help regardless of how they may have been individually gifted. On a *church* family level, routine or mundane tasks may involve opening up or locking down the building, mowing the grass, or cleaning the baptistry. Anyone who has the capability should help. Almost any adult would and should be able to lock and unlock the building by simply arriving early enough and staying late enough regardless of how God may have gifted them. However, when it comes to your "calling" ... your spiritual "niche" ... your *primary* place of service in the kingdom, this should be determined by how God has *gifted* you, not by what task needs doing or what position needs filling. *All* believers (not just seniors) would bless themselves, their church, and the recipients of all our collective ministry efforts far more richly if everyone was more in tune with how God has gifted them to serve in His kingdom. Our personal ministry efforts are so much more powerful when we're playing into our strengths (our giftedness) than when we're merely relying upon our natural capabilities.

Burnout

Burnout is a common problem not only in the business world but also in the lives of good-hearted, active, servant-minded believers. Victims of burnout may have been serving in a full-time, supported capacity, or simply as volunteers. There may be other factors as to why people experience burnout, but one of the reasons believers can experience *spiritual* or *ministry* burnout is because they're functioning primarily outside the arena of their giftedness. From a career perspective, a college graduate whose career opportunity takes him outside his actual field of education and passion can experience inordinate stress, excessive unhappiness, and eventual burnout. He may "make a living" from his job, but it might not be a good "fit," especially in the long haul. Similarly, when the primary ministry effort of a believer falls outside the arena of his true giftedness from God, joy can eventually be exchanged for duty, obligation, or even burnout.

81

This can occur even when that effort is for the noble cause of ministry if the believer is serving *outside* the arena of his true giftedness and God-intended place of ministry service. Educational backgrounds, personalities, and general abilities are transferable skills into other areas, but if the job (or the ministry task) isn't a fit, it simply isn't a fit, regardless of whether or not you have the capability to do it. Ironically, it is the transferability of such things as educational backgrounds, winning personalities, and general abilities in other areas that contribute to the situation. When we're ministering outside the arena of our giftedness, even ministry can become burdensome and exhausting, but when we're operating within the arena of our giftedness, even tiring service is an energizing joy.

Reactive vs. Proactive Ways to Identify And Address Needs and Potential

It's difficult to meet needs and use untapped potential that you don't even know exist. Hoping to meet the ministry needs of seniors and also tap into their potential without first carefully determining what and where their needs and potential lie is somewhat like a deer hunter walking through the woods, randomly firing his rifle and simply hoping a deer runs into the bullet. In other words, seniors ministry efforts with a vague or inadequate plan will miss many of the needs and potential of seniors. *Exceptional* seniors ministry requires that we be much more intentional (as intentional as we are with youth ministry) because exceptional ministry requires it.

The kind of assistance seniors need and the way to tap their potential can be addressed both proactively and reactively but is best addressed proactively. Those who work *reactively* with seniors wait until a need arises or reaches "critical mass" before they respond. With their reactive approach, they wait until unmet needs *finally* come to someone's attention which, in some cases, may never happen. Similarly, when it comes to *tapping potential*, those who work reactively with seniors wait for *seniors* to decide when and where or even whether to become involved in ministry service. With such a reactive approach, they expect less of seniors rather than more. Furthermore, when those who work reactively with seniors do try to tap the potential of seniors, they sometimes presume to utilize seniors with too little regard for how and where *God* may have intended them to serve in the kingdom *according to their giftedness*. In other words, reactive ministry with seniors waits and presumes.

On the other hand, those who work *proactively* with seniors don't wait and neither do they presume. Instead, they look for needs without waiting until someone or something *finally* brings that overlooked need to someone's attention. Those who work *proactively* with seniors don't wait until seniors may or may not volunteer to become involved in some ministry effort of the church. Rather, they seek the help of seniors or seek to help seniors discover (or reaffirm) how God has gifted them to serve. Then, they help enable and empower them to find how and where to exercise their giftedness in service to others. In other words, those who work *proactively* with seniors act preemptively and unpresumptuously. They ask, seek, and knock, rather than passively wait. They listen, observe, and anticipate, rather than presume.

Addressing the needs of seniors reactively rather than proactively is an inferior approach for any ministry, but it is especially inadequate for seniors ministry. It is inferior for two reasons. First, needs that are only addressed reactively are usually needs that have already gone unaddressed for a while and are only *finally* given attention. Responding reactively to the needs of seniors is not so much an "*If it ain't broke, don't fix it*" mentality as it is a "*What we don't know can't hurt us*" mindset. Try that philosophy out on the patient who is either unknowingly terminally ill or facing far more extensive and invasive treatment because the cancer went undetected due to negligence. What we don't know *can* hurt us. That's why it's good to have regular medical check-ups – to prevent problems and to catch problems early before they have an opportunity to become worse. Responding reactively to the ministry needs of seniors is better than nothing, but since when have churches and church leaders taken a "better than nothing" approach to ministry? Why would it be acceptable to take a more complacent, "better-than-nothing" approach to seniors ministry and yet consider it so unacceptable to take such a complacent "better than nothing" approach to youth ministry?

Another reason that the reactive approach to seniors ministry rather than the proactive approach is inferior is because needs that are met reactively tend to make the recipient feel like they're an *obligatory burden* on someone while needs that are met proactively help them feel it is a *joyful opportunity* for someone. The last thing independent-minded seniors need, who may already be incrementally losing their independence, is to be made to feel like a burden on others. Addressing the unmet needs of seniors is not just about addressing their needs. It's about addressing them in such a way that doesn't make seniors feel like a burden in the process. Providing assistance when seniors are lacking the ability is a step forward, but to do so in such a way that they've been made to feel they were an imposition is two or three steps backwards. What will eventually happen (and it won't take long) when seniors are made to feel like an imposition is that such seniors will simply stop making their needs known and will just allow their needs to go unmet. Not feeling like a burden to others is important to most seniors – a reality that should not be taken lightly.

Remember when earlier in this chapter I discussed visiting my mother to illustrate the value of assessing needs *relationally* (rather than formally through such means as an impersonal survey)? Those trips also illustrate the value of assessing needs *proactively* rather than reactively when addressing the fundamental needs of seniors. As you recall, my mother usually hesitates to make the "to do list" I ask her to make because she doesn't want to be an imposition. I use that hesitation, however, as an opportunity for reaffirmation by lovingly reassuring her of the honor and privilege that it genuinely is for me to do these things for her. The point is that I don't just work off of a reactive to do-list as would be done when relying on an impersonal survey approach for assessing needs. Rather, I *proactively* look for other needs that may have been excluded from the list whether accidentally or deliberately.

Sometimes a need may not have been included because it simply slipped her mind at the time she was compiling the list in preparation for my visit. Often though, it's because she doesn't want to feel like a burdensome imposition, so she intentionally keeps the list short. Sometimes it's because she's simply unaware of the need (i.e. the potentially dangerous wasp nest above the back porch entry, the low tire on the right rear side of her car, the leaky water faucet that increases utility bills unnecessarily). This simply underscores the importance of addressing the needs of seniors *proactively* with self-initiative rather than waiting for them to ask for help. However, what mostly underscores the value of how I meet my mother's needs is her typical *response* to such proactive help. On numerous occasions she has thanked me for not only doing the tasks but for doing them in such a way that didn't make her feel like she was causing some terrible imposition. In fact, she is probably more appreciative of *how* I do them (i.e. proactively, without making her feel like a burden) than she is that I actually do them.

Unless a seniors ministry program is primarily addressing the needs of seniors *proactively*, it constantly places them in the awkward position of either waiting until someone "finally" notices their needs or possibly never having their needs met. A reactive approach also tends to make seniors feel ashamed and embarrassed, or at least hesitant, when asking for help. When seniors are continually placed in such a situation, they become more and more discouraged from revealing their needs in the future.

SEVEN FUNDAMENTAL NEEDS OF SENIORS

#1 *Purposeful Living In Pre-Retirement And Retirement*
If the objective of churches and church leaders is to practice *exceptional* seniors ministry, they must begin with a better understanding of the needs of seniors which requires broadening our understanding of what those needs are for today's seniors. Only then can we begin addressing those needs exceptionally instead of so inadequately. The more clearly we identify their fundamental needs, the more effectively we can meet their needs. One of their fundamental needs is the need for purposeful living in pre-retirement and retirement. Beyond the proverbial "*food, shelter, and clothing,*" living life with purpose is one of the most fundamental needs of anyone. This is especially true for seniors who often struggle to live with continued purpose once they've reached the empty nest and career retirement stages of life.

Even though the length of life is "*as a vapor that appears briefly and then vanishes*" (Jm. 4:14), God made us to live the time we have on earth ... all of it ... with purpose and meaning. It's in the "DNA" of our spirit and soul. Trying to live our life without meaning and purpose is like trying to live our life without eating or breathing – it causes serious problems. It's like trying to drive a car while depriving it of one of the fluids necessary to keep it running properly. Drive a car without oil in the engine, transmission fluid in the transmission, water in the radiator, or brake fluid in the brake cylinders and the car will eventually self-destruct. The manufacturer designed a car to have these fluids. Our "Manufacturer" designed us to live purposeful, meaningful lives. Whenever that's missing in our life, things begin to go wrong. At the very least, they don't go as well as God desires and intends for us.

Today's seniors are living longer and are healthier than ever, thanks to a number of factors (better nutrition, better medications, better medical knowledge, and better surgical procedures). Back in the "good ole days," when we didn't have the benefits of these advancements in science and medicine, more people died at a younger age, leaving less time for what we now call the retirement years. My mother's dad died when my mother was a fourteen month old toddler, and her mother died when she was only ten. Her parents never faced struggling with having or keeping a purpose in life during their senior years. They were in the middle of raising a family, making a living, and trying to build a future.

Today's seniors live in a different world. Seventy-five years is now the average lifespan of a man and 80 years is the average for a woman (according to 2004 statistics). Some sources suggest even longer. Consequently, as seniors reach their "retirement" years in their 60s or 70s (and some retire in their late 50s), they can still have 10 to 20 or more years left to live. That's a long time to live without purpose or meaning. As a rule, previous generations of seniors didn't face such a situation. This presents today's seniors with either a dilemma or an opportunity, depending on whether you're the kind of person who looks at a half a glass of water and sees it "half empty" or "half full." The obligations and the opportunities churches and church leaders have are to recognize this fundamental need of seniors and to develop a seniors ministry program that addresses this need. It's also important to realize that for more and more of today's seniors the challenge of living a purposeful life can begin prior to a senior's traditionally perceived "retirement" years. An exceptional seniors ministry program will anticipate this, too.

#2 *Relevancy And Significance In A Youth-Focused Culture*
A second fundamental ministry need of seniors that is closely related to the need for purposeful living is the need for relevancy and significance in a youth-focused culture. If purposeful living is the *what,* relevancy and significance is the *how.* If you've ever been in a situation where you've felt completely irrelevant, you know how worthless and insignificant that can make you feel. You don't have to be a

senior to become "out of touch" with life around you, but seniors are especially in danger of becoming seemingly irrelevant and insignificant unless an intentional effort is made by seniors themselves and others who care enough to make it a joint effort.

We live in a fast-changing world where the latest, greatest "hip" and "chic" clothes fashions quickly become out of style. Similarly, rapidly changing technology makes the technology within today's cutting edge computers "dinosaurs" in 6-12 months – if not before they even hit the stores! As a rule, youth have no trouble keeping up with the fast pace of today's world. In fact, they usually thrive on it. However, seniors can easily become "antiques" in a youth-focused culture, but only if they choose to do so ... and only if churches and church leaders allow it by choosing to do nothing to proactively help seniors remain relevant and significant. Playing golf, puttering around the house, and traveling on vacation eventually "wear thin" when it comes to living a meaningful life. When such life-altering events as the empty nest, job retirement, and gradually diminishing health begin to enter the picture, the need for relevancy and significance, though just as essential as ever, can become deeply threatened.

If we care about the ministry needs of today's seniors, we should value and seek their wisdom and input by discovering their areas of interest, skills, and experience. Then, we should pro-actively partner with them to find ways to channel their time and energy in meaningful service to others. Younger generations should invite and include seniors into their own areas of ministry interest, too. Proactive efforts should be made to discover the strengths of seniors and then to sincerely tell them how much their strengths are valued. We must, however, do more than merely *verbalize* the value we hold for seniors. We must *demonstrate* how much we value seniors by utilizing their strengths!

A senior's relevancy and significance can be maintained by such things as continual education and intergenerational activities. The moment seniors become content with relying on the past - outdated technology, outdated activities, or outdated relationships (i.e. only past memories) is the moment their continued relevancy and significance becomes endangered. Similarly, the moment churches and church leaders become content with relying on the past (outdated methods, outdated activities, outdated paradigms for seniors ministry) is the moment they start adding to this problem. The horse and buggy may still be a quaint and novel activity to experience, but it's usually something done only once or twice on some special occasion for recreational amusement. Other than for this, the horse and buggy in our society is as irrelevant as it is insignificant – something few take seriously anymore.

Society required that the phonograph give way to the 8 track tape and the 8 track tape to the cassette. Then, the cassette gave way to the CD and the CD to the HD (hard drive) just to remain relevant and significant in a fast-paced and ever-changing world. Seniors must likewise learn to embrace new things. Some seniors are better at maintaining relevancy on their own, but for many, this requires a way to help encourage, enable, and empower them to remain so. Otherwise, we will be leaving seniors behind in the ash heaps of irrelevancy and insignificance unnecessarily.

#3 *Reassurance In Times Of Discouragement*
A third fundamental ministry need of seniors is reassurance in times of discouragement. Although the need for encouragement is certainly not unique to seniors, we are seemingly not as mindful of this need among seniors as we are with younger generations, as reflected by the lack of time, attention, and resources allocated to seniors ministry. It's not that seniors are totally ignored or never encouraged but rather that they are only given minimal encouragement, while other groups are given maximum encouragement. Bible class lessons and sermons are helpful, but like children and teens or young and middle-age adults, seniors also need encouraging reassurance on a more personal and frequent basis.

If we care about the ministry needs of today's seniors, we should be making organized ministry efforts that build relationships with seniors so that we can know when and why senior members are in need of reassurance. If we care about the ministry needs of today's seniors, we should be spending enough time with them to not only notice but to even *sense* when they are discouraged and in need of encouragement. Exceptional seniors ministry requires being routinely involved sufficiently and closely enough in the lives of senior members to know what's going on in their lives. It requires knowing when to offer those words of encouragement, as well as how best to provide them with support and assistance when needed.

The difference between the kind and amount of encouragement given to younger generations and that which is given to seniors is the difference between proactive encouragement and reactive encouragement. The kind of encouragement we provide for our youth comes in the form of a proactive, first class, fully funded, highly creative, and very innovative youth ministry program led by a full-time staff person. However, the kind of encouragement we all too often provide for seniors is typically a reactive, third class, under-funded, predictable, occasional "here-and-there" activity led by volunteers.

Where we routinely provide other ages with proactive encouragement, the kind of encouragement we routinely provide seniors seems to mostly come in the form of reactive financial assistance when they can't pay a bill, reactive visits when they're sick or in the hospital, and reactive moral support after the death of a spouse. It's not that reactive encouragement is bad. It's just that there is little if any proactive encouragement. Whatever proactive encouragement may exist is disproportionately less than what is devoted to other ministry efforts which we consider "important." Such a disproportionate and inequitable response reveals just how astonishingly out of touch we are about the need for proactive encouragement with seniors. It would seem that we simply don't "get it" that seniors also need proactive encouragement.

Just to be clear, we're not talking about providing seniors with a youth ministry program. We're not talking about treating seniors like "*15 year old teens with 50 years experience.*" It would be as misguided to provide seniors with a style better suited for youth ministry as it would be to provide youth with a style better suited for seniors ministry. Ironically, this was what was done with teens in years past. Many churches only offered our youth "traditional" Sunday school classes and adult assemblies until we finally realized that this was no longer adequately meeting the ministry needs of our youth. Just as we eventually moved beyond yesterday's solutions for ministry with today's youth, we need to move beyond yesterday's solutions for ministry with today's seniors. This includes and requires transitioning from reactive to proactive encouragement.

#4 *Assistance When Lacking Ability*
A fourth fundamental ministry need of seniors is assistance when they lack ability. This is especially true for those who are older but still living independently. Most seniors are a fiercely independent bunch. At least they want to be for as long as possible. Self reliance and independence can be good if not driven by pride or taken to extremes. This country was founded upon "rugged individualism." Our founding forefathers signed a Declaration of *In*dependence – not a Declaration of *De*pendence. Although our American culture has always demonstrated an exceptional willingness to help others in need (nationally and internationally), we generally and desperately want to be on the ingratiating *giving* end, rather than the indebted *receiving* end of that assistance. Even Jesus said that "*It is more blessed to give than to receive*" (Acts 20:35). In more recent years, that fierce, independent spirit seems to be incrementally dissipating with each younger American generation. Well-intended but often misguided or abused government aid programs have only promoted a growing dependency. However, seniors are still among those from the "old school" who are more determined to rely on themselves as much and as long as possible rather than become dependent upon others.

The majority of today's seniors want to live in their own houses for as long as possible rather than live in community with other seniors – *regardless* of how nice the facility may be or how many amenities it has to offer. They want to keep a car and to continue driving (or at least have that option) for as long as possible rather than be shuttled around in a van by someone else. They want to buy their own groceries with their own money rather than have to rely upon food stamps and other welfare programs. Many want to make their own end-of-life decisions rather than have someone else (even a close family member) make such decisions for them. Those making ministry efforts with today's seniors must be cognizant of this strong tendency among seniors. Ironically, their independent nature contributes to, compounds, and exacerbates the reason why we fail to as readily see the need for developing an exceptional seniors ministry program. When we are already less mindful of their ministry needs than we are with other age groups, the independent nature of seniors only further masks their needs.

As the old axiom says *"The squeaky wheel gets the grease."* This creates a predicament. Either godly seniors can begin "squeaking" loudly about their unmet ministry needs (which is against their very independent nature), or they can remain silent about their unmet ministry needs. Given the unimposing nature of godly seniors, we will apparently continue overlooking and under-serving their ministry needs until those who care about seniors begin speaking up on their behalf. Seniors who were once more independent, but now require some assistance are particularly vulnerable to being overlooked and unnoticed. Meeting the needs of such seniors requires the kind of attention that best comes from close, caring relatives, neighbor friends, and *personally involved church members.*

If we seriously care about the ministry needs of today's seniors, we should establish exceptional ministry efforts that include making those daily phone calls and regularly having those friendly need-revealing chats. Better yet (without having to be told or asked), we should drop by and discover the need to move that fallen tree limb from the yard or the need to change that ceiling light bulb in the kitchen. When we discover that the thought of a trip to the supermarket, pharmacy, or mall has become so intimidating that some seniors simply stay home, we can invite them to go with us. This can not only provide them with the needed help, it also builds a relationship and can even turn the trip into an enjoyable adventure for them.

#5 *Needed For Meaningful Service*

A fifth fundamental ministry need of seniors is to be needed for meaningful service. The more we allow our youth-focused culture to squeeze seniors into the world's "retirement" mentality mold, the more seniors will be made to feel unneeded. There are few feelings more hurtful and discouraging than the feeling of being unneeded. Like the first and second fundamental needs mentioned earlier in this chapter, this fifth need also acknowledges the importance of purpose, relevancy, and significance in the life of a senior, but in a distinctive way. The key word here is *meaningful.* It's not enough to simply find things for seniors to do. They must be encouraged and empowered to serve in ways that are personally fulfilling.

Being Authentically Needed vs. Being Merely Patronized

A crucial distinction must be made between a senior *being* authentically needed and a senior artificially being made to merely *feel* needed in a well-intended but condescending and patronizing way. Exceptional seniors ministry requires having an *authentic* need for seniors. I'm not talking about "busy work" tasks where all that's being accomplished is to *"help the poor ole thing feel useful."* I'm not talking about

89

tasks to merely "*give them something to do*" or "*keep them occupied*" or "*out of trouble*" or "*out of my hair.*" At the same time, menial tasks should not be beneath a senior ... any more than they should be beneath anyone else. Neither is it a bad thing to want to help someone *feel* useful or give them something to do to keep them occupied or out from under foot. It's just that these should be incidental or secondary benefits rather than the primary motive or objective.

Shallow motivation betrays a condescending, patronizing attitude that merely affirms a perspective that seniors really are unneeded. Seniors can readily and easily sense such an attitude. Until we can escape that fundamentally flawed perception about seniors by *genuinely* recognizing the value of what they have to offer, we will help hold seniors captive in a prison cell called "unneeded." The truth of the matter is, seniors have much to offer. However, we have been so focused on other good ministry efforts that we haven't spent nearly enough time, attention, and resources on seniors ministry to seriously explore, much less discover and plan in detail or with much creativity and innovation, how to utilize what seniors have to offer in the way of meaningful service.

Busy Work vs. Meaningful Service

Just as seniors have the need to be *genuinely* needed, they also have the need to be genuinely needed for *meaningful* service. It's not enough to be needed. This fundamental ministry need also includes and involves *what* seniors are needed for and *why* they are needed. Effectively addressing this fundamental need of seniors is not merely about making seniors "feel" needed. It's also about *genuinely* needing and utilizing their skills, wisdom, and availability in ways that are perceived *by them* as meaningful. Seniors should not merely become the "dumping ground" for all the routine and mundane tasks of the church but should be empowered for what they perceive as meaningful service.

If our approach to meeting their need to be needed only entails "busywork" or "odds and ends" with little regard for how God has gifted seniors for service or for whether such tasks would be meaningful to them, such seniors ministry efforts have fundamentally failed at meeting this fifth fundamental need. Any question about how well seniors may be able to handle "important" tasks is an understandable but very revealing concern. It reveals a hint of lingering "ageism." It also indicates that we still haven't really grasped the concept of helping seniors discover their *giftedness* and *place of service* in the kingdom.

Concern for whether seniors are competent for more than mere menial tasks indicates that we are not yet concerned enough about helping seniors discover or reaffirm how God has gifted seniors to serve. If we have helped seniors identify their authentic giftedness from God and place of service in the kingdom, concern that seniors may or may not be competent for the task becomes irrelevant. If they are exercising their giftedness from God, it's a foregone conclusion that they will be competent. Even if there is room for improvement through additional training, further education, and additional experience (as there would be for members of any age), they *will* be both qualified and competent if their giftedness has been accurately identified.

One Man's Trash

When it comes to addressing the fundamental need of seniors to be needed for meaningful service, how "important" the task may be perceived by others may be irrelevant in comparison to how meaningful the task is to that senior. As the old saying goes, *"One man's trash is another man's treasure."* What may seem unimportant or less important to one person may be very important to another. What one person may find mundane, another may consider surprisingly meaningful. To illustrate, I spoke with an entrepreneurial friend of mine recently who was about to go on vacation when a new business opportunity unexpectedly presented itself to him. Before he could make a commitment about this new potential venture, he had to "crunch some numbers" to confirm its profitability.

As we stood in his front yard and talked before he left for a two week vacation, he said he planned to spend some of his vacation time crunching those numbers. For him, crunching numbers is enjoyable and relaxing. He wasn't "under the gun" with some deadline that was requiring him to compromise his vacation time. He *wanted* to crunch those numbers! He *enjoyed* crunching numbers! He said it was *relaxing* for him to crunch numbers! It would drive me crazy to spend vacation time crunching numbers. For him, however, it's relaxing to ruminate and meditate with God on another potential business opportunity from a low-key, no hassle perspective in a vacation setting.

One man's trash truly is another man's treasure. Meeting this fifth fundamental need doesn't necessarily require relying on seniors to do "important" tasks (although it shouldn't exclude them either!), but it does require more than merely patronizing, condescending busywork just to make someone feel needed. If we are serious about authentically addressing the fundamental ministry need of seniors to be needed for meaningful service, then the service opportunities found and provided for seniors in an exceptional seniors ministry program require identifying and utilizing their giftedness while also finding and providing opportunities for *meaningful* service in whatever form that may take.

#6 *Intergenerational Friendships And Fellowship*

A sixth fundamental ministry need of seniors is for intergenerational friendships and fellowship. There are so many important things that churches and church leaders need to re-think, unlearn, and learn anew when it comes to seniors ministry. This is one of the "big ones." When seniors ministry is just about seniors, it's inclined to become little more than an "old folks social club" that few people (including seniors!) want to have anything to do with at all. When seniors ministry is only about seniors, it can become a virtual subculture within the church.

It simply should not be considered adequate expressions of friendship and fellowship for younger believers to only have a few superficial acquaintances with older generations. Neither should it be considered sufficient outreach to simply sit in a church pew next to someone older or merely exchange brief pleasantries with them in the foyer on Sundays. Because of our culture that encourages a "retirement" mentality, many seniors slowly begin to withdraw from life as they grow older. If we care about seriously addressing the ministry needs of today's seniors, we must encourage and cultivate close and active friendships between seniors and younger generations.

The friendship and fellowship of younger generations with seniors is the flip side to meeting their needs when they are lacking ability. Just like meeting their needs can be accomplished by such things as frequent phone calls and regular visits to their home, friendships and fellowship can be encouraged and cultivated by making such efforts as having seniors in your home, inviting them to the movies with your family, including them in a family picnic or outing, and other relationship building activities.

Specializationism

Just as God is good at taking a bad thing and making good come from it, Satan is good at taking a good thing and making bad come from it. Ultimately, God wins this battle of good and evil, but Satan can wreak much havoc along the way, causing unnecessary detours, delays, and damage. We have become a culture of specialists. While God has made good use of this, Satan has done a good job of turning it to our disadvantage, especially when it comes to seniors ministry. As a general rule, specialization is a good thing, but it can have its drawbacks. Thanks to such rapid and massive advancements in knowledge and technology, specialization has, in fact, become a necessity. No one person can learn, know, or do it all. We can become a master of something or a "jack of all trades," but nobody can become a master of all things. If you want the best heart or brain surgeon, you'd better not rely on a general practitioner.

There was a time when "the local preacher" did it all. He preached sermons, taught classes, led the youth ministry program, wrote books, designed the class curriculum, did radio programs, wrote newspaper articles, emceed all the church events, married and buried members, counseled troubled lives and marriages ... and more. He was a one man band ... a "jack of all trades" who was expected to be the master of all. In a less specialized world, he could "pull it off" ... or at least appear to do so. However, just as the medical field has become highly specialized, which is a good thing, so have the ministry efforts and activities of churches, which is also a good thing. Specialization, though, has a downside. Gone are the days in many places where the family sits together regularly and "does church" intergenerationally as a family. Now we have "children's church" and "teen worship centers" that specialize in focusing on the age-specific needs of younger generations.

Specialization To The Detriment Of Seniors

We have so compartmentalized our church ministry efforts and activities that the opportunity for (and even a desire for) intergenerational friendship and fellowship has been significantly diminished. Granted, efforts are made that invite and include all ages, but it's usually more of a heterogeneous experience without homogeneous results, where substantially more "spiritual fusion" actually needs to occur among the different ages. A cook, for example, can "mix" water and oil by pouring them into the same container, but it doesn't mean any "bonding" has occurred between the two elements. However, if you mix a tablespoon of water to a half cup of cooking oil along with some other ingredients such as flour, eggs, and milk and then bake those ingredients in the "fellowship" of a warm oven over a period of time, something special happens. When thoroughly mixed together and with time together in the oven, these individual ingredients can beautifully and deliciously turn into something that is far more valuable and useful bonded together than when these ingredients are merely occupying the same space but remaining apart or when merely mixed together but only in a heterogeneous state. Similarly, we can place seniors at the same place and time with younger generations, but it doesn't guarantee that any relational "bonding" occurs between the two different generations.

Since the Garden of Eden, when the first family unit arrived on the scene, God declared the value of intergenerational relationships. Thousands of years later, long after God had originally "staked out His position" on the matter, He apparently hadn't change His mind because God, through Paul, was still advising the "*older women to teach the younger women*" (Tit. 2). Intergenerational friendships and fellowship can play a significantly positive role in the spiritual, emotional, and social well being of all believers but this is especially true for senior believers. I say "can" rather than "does" because it only *does* if we proactively encourage it.

Mutually Beneficial

Intergenerational friendships and fellowship have benefits for *all* generations. It's a two-way street for everyone involved, not a one-way street exclusively for seniors. Younger generations need seniors. There are things God cannot do for younger generations without seniors. There are lessons younger generations will not learn when and how God wants them learned (i.e. sooner rather than later, and the "easy" way instead of the "hard" way) without seniors. More importantly, there is shaping and molding that God cannot do for younger generations without seniors. Seniors play a valuable role in the welfare of others in ways that are sometimes more readily recognizable ... and sometimes in ways which are not as obvious. Whenever I speak of the value of seniors and what they have to offer to younger generations, it is the *godly* senior who is always presumed. It's a given that it's the *godly* senior who has the most value to offer others. The mere number of candles on the cake is no guarantee of anything other than an individual's chronological age.

A Blessing To Grandchildren

One of the more obvious examples of the value of intergenerational interaction is between godly grandparents and their grandchildren, or with other children to whom they can serve as a "grandfatherly" or "grandmotherly" figure. Just as there are things that even godly grandparents cannot offer a child that only godly parents can, there are things that godly parents cannot offer a child that only godly grandparents can provide. Godly grandparents can play an invaluable and irreplaceable role in the life of a child. However, as significant and important a role as godly grandparenting is, seniors are good for so much more than only grandparenting.

A Blessing To Younger Adults

Their very presence can be a "rock" of stability for a younger adult whose life may feel like it's spinning out of control. Seniors can be a stabilizing force for those who may be facing a crisis they've never faced before but that some senior has faced and is living proof that you can come out on the other side. Seniors can be a listening ear for a troubled heart. They can be an example and an inspiration to a troubled marriage by demonstrating that marriages truly can weather the storms of life and last a lifetime. Seniors can add insight and wisdom to a less experienced soul – and in doing so, can enrich the lives of others in the seemingly smallest (and yet most significant) of ways.

Me, Myself, And I

Although I am not yet considered "senior" by most standards, I am by AARP's definition because I'm over 50 years old. In the eyes of newlyweds I am a senior since I have been happily married for nearly 35 years. I once attended a weekend men's retreat that was a mix of men of all ages. By mere chance (actually, it was by the Spirit's leading), I happened to sit next to a young man in the dining hall during some unstructured free time between activities. As I struck up what I originally intended to be merely casual conversation, I couldn't help but notice the preoccupied and deeply troubled look on this young man's face. When I asked if there was something on his mind, he began to open up about his troubled marriage. He had only been married for a couple of years. As I listened, he explained how he was longing to give his wife a call right then and there during the retreat, but was struggling to put his feelings into words. As he continued to talk, he proceeded to tell me how much *he* missed her, how much *he* couldn't live without her, and how badly *he* felt about their estrangement. I couldn't help but notice how his deeply troubled soul seemed far more focused on himself rather than upon her, so I shared that observation with him.

As I spoke those words, you could literally "see the lights come on," judging from the expression on his face. He immediately "got it." He wasn't *trying* to be self-focused, but in all his pain he was simply more focused on his own wounded and hurting self than he was upon his wounded and hurting wife. I suggested that if he had called her while he was so focused on *his* pain, he would probably have driven her even further away. This young man literally jumped up from the table where we were sitting and gave me a hearty hug while enthusiastically reaching for his cell phone to call his wife. That day, God saw to it that our paths crossed because He knew the blessing an older adult could be to a younger adult. Seniors can be a blessing to others in the most unexpected ways when intergenerational friendships and fellowship are cultivated and encouraged.

Legendary Pies

My mother is a great cook and my dad loved to eat. I recall her sharing a story about her "trial and error" days when they were newlyweds. Shortly after she and my dad married, my mother made a pecan pie. As a newlywed, my mother's efforts had far more tender loving care than they did experience. My dad didn't care for the pie and it broke my mother's heart ... but not her spirit or her determination. Today, her reputation for pecan pies as well as all her fruit and pudding pies still made with "homemade from scratch" crusts is widely known. They are relished not only within the family but also among relatives, in-laws, neighbors and her entire home church family. Whereas some might not want to share such favorite recipes with others, my mother has freely shared many of hers so that other, younger wives and mothers could become "legendary" in their families and among their own friends.

Legendary Rolls

I recall my grandmother doing something similar for my mother many years ago. My mother could make some of the most incredibly delicious "homemade light bread" imaginable. As a child, I would watch, time and again, with anticipation as she kneaded the bread and let it rise – and kneaded it again to allow it to rise several times before finally placing a pan of rolls in the oven to cook until golden brown. The smell of the rolls as they were cooking was tantalizing. The taste was *"to die for,"* especially when a little butter was added to the rolls just as they came out of the oven. However, as absolutely delicious as those fresh-out-of-the-oven rolls always tasted, they were never quite as "light" as my grandmother's rolls, even though my mother used the exact same recipe and allowed the dough to rise the same number of times. This was especially perplexing to my mother since, by this time, she had become such an exceptionally good cook.

It bothered my mother for years that she couldn't figure out the difference. She used the exact same recipe and ingredients that my grandmother used. She observed how the ingredients were mixed. She cut the dough the same size for each roll. She carefully observed how my grandmother kneaded the dough. She tried to eliminate any and all variables. She even made bread in the presence of my grandmother in hopes of discovering some subtle difference in the course of cooking together. Still, my grandmother's rolls were noticeably lighter (not tastier, but lighter) than my mother's. Finally one day, my mother point blank asked my grandmother why her rolls turned out a little lighter. My grandmother said she had never wanted to say anything because she didn't want to hurt my mother's feelings or come across sounding like some "bossy" and overbearing in-law. The answer she gave that was the "secret" to her rolls being lighter was stunningly simple. My grandmother said all she did differently was place fewer dough rolls in the pan, so they would have a little more room to expand one last time while baking! As a mother of two bread-loving sons and wife of a husband who loved to eat, my mother had always unwittingly placed as many rolls as possible in the pan.

This seemingly small and insignificant "secret" that was freely and humbly shared with my mother by her mother-in-law was one of many things this older senior did to bless a young daughter-in-law. More significantly, the value my grandmother was that day to my mother went beyond simply learning how to make lighter homemade bread. It further endeared an already close relationship between two generations. In fact, it reached beyond those generations. The blessing my grandmother was to my mother was likewise passed on by my mother to my wife who, in turn, has also shared the "secret" to lighter, homemade rolls.

A Blessing To Seniors

The value and benefits of intergenerational friendships and fellowship, however, are a two-way street, as noted earlier. Younger generations are not the only ones who are blessed. Seniors also benefit tremendously. There is at least as much value and benefit for seniors to have friendships and fellowship with younger generations as there is for younger generations to have friendships and fellowship with seniors. Businesses and sports teams can often benefit from bringing in rookies to provide "fresh blood" to an organization. In a similar way the interaction of seniors with younger generations has something of value to offer that fellowship merely with other seniors can't provide.

Seniors need to be reminded on an intellectual, relational, and experiential level about the childlike nature of life. This can perhaps best be experienced through interaction with children. Seniors need to be reminded about *seeing* life through unjaded eyes and *living* life enthusiastically through interaction with teenagers. They need to be reminded about living life with meaning and purpose through friendships and fellowship with young and middle-age adults who have a strong sense of mission, purpose, and objective in life. A seniors ministry program that intentionally, proactively, energetically, and regularly encourages intergenerational friendships and fellowship with each of these age groups is one that ensures this sixth fundamental ministry need is being adequately addressed.

96

#7 *Grace-Based Relationship With God*

The seventh and last fundamental ministry need of seniors that we'll consider is a grace-based relationship with God. Many of today's seniors grew up in an age when the laws of God were probably emphasized far more than the grace of God. Consequently, they may not have been given as much assurance of the grace of God as He has always intended for us. Let me be clear that it's not a matter of law *vs.* grace. It's not a matter of either/or but *both*. We don't have to choose one or the other. It's just that when one is emphasized more than the other or one to the neglect of the other, we can have a lopsided perspective of God, our relationship with Him, and our eternal security. Unless we have a *balanced* understanding of the grace and law of God, the imbalance can result in a significant spiritual deficiency either in assurance or reality.

There is a direct correlation between a limited grasp of the grace of God and the peaceful assurance that may be lacking in a conscientious but troubled heart. Similarly, there is a direct correlation between a limited grasp of the laws of God and the consequences of willful disrespect for God's will. Our access to the generous grace of God and our unwavering allegiance to the absolute laws of God is one of many *seemingly* irreconcilable dichotomies in scripture. I would not claim to fully comprehend, much less adequately explain, how these two seemingly mutually exclusive spiritual principles can co-exist in complete harmony in the mind of God, but they do, according to scripture. We must simply, wholeheartedly, and equally embrace both.

Pendulum Extremes

In today's *younger* generations, I fear the pendulum may have swung too far in *the other direction where there is the need for a better law-inclusive relationship* with God. Paul addressed this *"anything goes"* attitude about Christian living long ago when writing to believers who were a little too "graced-based happy" and not enough "law-inclusive grounded." He rhetorically asked, *"Shall we continue in sin that grace may abound? God forbid!"* (Rom. 6:1, 2). I fear that as many of today's more "touchy-feely" grace-based youth become adults, unless they come to a deeper respect and appreciation for the laws of God, they may find themselves suffering opposite consequences. They may find themselves facing the consequences of living with too little regard for the word of God and the consequences of behavior contrary to the will of God. Whenever such disrespect for God's laws persists, it's only a matter of time before we'll eventually experience a "reality check."

Internalizing The Grace Of God

However, today's *seniors* were raised when what was likely emphasized most was God's law. In order to help bring that lop-sided emphasis into balance, what they probably need most is greater assurance about grace. As seniors near the end of their lives, God's intention for them and for all His children, even in the midst of all our imperfections, is to have *"blessed assurance"* that *"when the roll is called up yonder I'll be there."* If merely saying or singing such words of confidence were all it took to genuinely feel that way, everything would be just fine. If merely verbalizing such sentiments were all that was necessary to give us the peaceful assurance that God longs and intends for all of His children to have, even in the midst of our imperfections, we could approach the end of our life and face even death without doubts, concern, or fear. However, if the laws of God were deeply imbedded into our soul during the formative years of our life without an equal emphasis on the grace of God, it will likely require more than a little "self talk" to internalize needed assurances about our relationship with God and our eternal security.

By the time the senior years of life arrive, even believers have lived nearly an entire life that has been stained with wrong choices, missteps, bad decisions, mistakes, and regrets. For some, those mistakes are more frequent and significant than for others. It may be regrets about how we raised our children or how much more "quality time" we should have spent with them. It may be regrets about a divorce or regrets about misplaced priorities. It may be regrets about addictions or abuse. It may be regrets about broken relationships or regrets about our sins in general. Without a grace-based relationship with God, the heart of even a "church going" believer can become very heavy and may lose or doubt the hope which God extends to all of his children. Time and again I've known of even godly seniors who were less than blessedly assured about the certainty of their eternal destiny. Sometimes, they seem to have a tentative kind of assurance that resembles more of a *"whistling in the dark while walking past a graveyard at midnight."* In their heart of hearts, they weren't really all that sure if they would really be there when the roll is called up yonder.

For today's seniors who may find themselves in this situation, there is a need to reach out in ministry efforts that will help them. There is a need to help such seniors gain a better understanding of and fuller appreciation for the grace of God. When you've been raised in an age when *"hellfire and damnation"* and "commandment keeping" were given far more emphasis by well-intended preachers and teachers than the grace of God, God's grace is not an easy lesson to genuinely internalize. It may be easy to *profess* or to *sing* about the peaceful assurance that God's grace offers, but when we're nearing the end of our lives it can be a difficult spiritual truth for some to truly *internalize*. Grace-based assurance is a lesson far more easily *intellectually learned* than *actually internalized* because legalism is a difficult lesson to unlearn.

The other side of the coin, ironically, is that seniors who have had a legalistic spiritual upbringing may need a better understanding of grace for yet another reason. They may need a better understanding of God's grace to move beyond a false assurance grounded more in prideful, meritorious law-keeping that essentially "earns" your way to security of heaven through such things as "faithful" church attendance, doing good deeds, and keeping God's commandments. Either way, the fundamental need of seniors for a grace-based relationship with God is one that should not be overlooked or under-emphasized if we're interested in addressing this fundamental need of seniors.

CHAPTER SEVEN
When The Tail Wags The Dog
(outreach to seniors)

What you do think when you hear the word *outreach* in the context of ministry? Although there may be no deliberate attempt to consciously and intentionally exclude an individual or group of individuals, few would likely think of outreach to seniors. As evidenced by many church programs and budgets, when we think about outreach we tend to primarily think about teens, children, young families, middle-age families, self-help recovery groups, divorcees, and so forth. Unfortunately, we're probably not really thinking much about outreach to seniors. We may think about the unchurched, the overchurched, the underchurched, single parents, and addicts, but we're probably not really thinking much about outreach to seniors. We may think about prostitutes, abortionists, homosexuals, post-moderns, foreign missions, and the "lost" in general, but if we're honest with ourselves we're probably not really thinking much about outreach to seniors. Outreach to seniors just doesn't readily come to mind. There may be other explanations as to why we generally don't think of seniors when thinking of outreach in the community, but one underlying contributing factor is our flawed emphasis about *building up membership,* and another is our defective thinking about *results* in ministry.

A Bad Case of "Growth-itis"

It's understandable that every church leadership wants their church to grow in numbers. There's nothing "wrong" with this. In fact, there's something very right about a church growing in numbers. The early church grew by leaps and bounds at times. On the day of Pentecost, the church grew by 3,000 souls after just one sermon (Acts 2:41) and they experienced numerical growth on a daily basis as well (Acts 2:47). Only a short time later, the Jerusalem church grew by yet another 2,000 (Acts 4:4). The early church experienced explosive, exponential numerical growth like most churches today can only dream about doing. To experience such growth, whether by actual conversion or even by mere "brick shifting" would be any church's dream.

The problematic side of church growth occurs when "the tail begins to wag the dog." Even the best of churches and church leaders cannot help but keep a watchful eye on the numbers. With such realities as massive building payments, staff salaries, spiraling utilities, building maintenance, facility improvements and expansion, and numerous ministry program obligations all continually breathing down their collective necks, church leaders undoubtedly find it difficult not to focus on numbers. Then there's the pride factor. What group of church leaders wouldn't want to be considered at least partially responsible for causing a church to grow? However, there's a huge difference between church growth that occurs because leaders are carefully following the prescribed strategies of some church growth guru and church growth that occurs because leaders trust in God's prescribed priorities. The former relies on the wisdom of man while the other trusts in the wisdom, power, and faithfulness of God.

Church Growth Gurus vs. God's Priorities?

Eventually ... perhaps inevitably that tail does begin wagging the dog. Eventually ... perhaps subconsciously and unintentionally ministry effort decisions are influenced more by concerns for church growth than concerns for God's priorities. I fear too many churches and church leaders may be paying almost worshipful attention to what well known and highly respected church growth gurus have to say about church growth in today's world. No doubt there is much wisdom in what these church growth experts have to say. In fact, we would be wise to give serious consideration to their advice. However, if such church growth advice *excludes* any of God's priorities by failing to include those priorities in their recommendations, these experts ultimately do churches and church leaders a grave disservice.

If there are certain things churches can begin doing or improve upon based upon the recommendations of outside consultants, we should take full advantage of their insights. Such advice about church growth can serve us well as long as their insights don't provide justification to knowingly neglect or minimize any of God's priorities such as seniors ministry. The problem is, that's *exactly* what happens. Even if it's an unintended consequence, unintentional consequences can be just as consequential as intentioned ones.

From a church growth guru's perspective, advising churches and church leaders to begin making ministry with seniors a high priority will not likely happen because it simply doesn't fit today's church growth template. However, such church growth advice neither changes nor diminishes God's high priority for seniors ministry. The *primary* objective of a church growth consultant is not to honor God's specified priority about seniors but rather to offer insights and advice on growing churches from a strategic and tactical point of view. Otherwise, they'd be known as church *priority* consultants instead of church *growth* consultants. Furthermore, their recommendations to churches would typically include treating seniors ministry more like a high priority than an afterthought. This is not to say church growth experts are intentionally antagonistic toward God's high priority for seniors. Neither is it

101

intended to be harsh and judgmental toward them. It's simply to acknowledge the obvious ... that their *primary* objective is not about priorities but growth.

In fact, if we would just take an objective step back and see the future status of the church from God's perspective, we would realize that the very notion of a need to focus on church "growth" hints of off-target and misplaced priorities. Didn't the Apostle Paul say to focus on the planting and watering because God takes care of the increase (1 Cor. 3:6)? When we make ministry program decisions based more on numbers and results than we do upon God's priorities, we need to realign our priorities with the priorities of God. When numbers become more important than God's priorities, it's time to reconsider what's more important to God – numerical growth or honoring His priorities.

The Future Of The Church?

On a similar note, the main reason usually expressed for the emphasis we place on youth ministry is *"they're the future of the church."* That's actually thinking about church growth instead of thinking about God's priorities! It's arrogant thinking to even subconsciously presume that the future of the church actually depends upon us rather than upon God. As shocking and politically incorrect as it may sound, God doesn't need youth ministry to preserve the future of the church. While some may be reeling in shock and gasping for breath as they struggle for oxygen to declare anathema on such a "heretical" statement, let me repeat it for emphasis. God doesn't need youth ministry to preserve the future of the church ... any more than He needed the children of Abraham to preserve His chosen race of people (Mt. 3:9).

If God, as John the Baptizer fierily thundered, can *"raise up children for Abraham"* out of mere rocks scattered on the ground, then surely He doesn't need youth ministry programs to preserve the future of the church. He may choose to use youth ministry like He can choose to use *any* ministry program, but He doesn't *need* them to preserve "the future of the church." The point is not to "dis" youth or youth ministry, but to help clear our clouded thinking by establishing an objective perspective and a healthy reminder that we are not in the church growth business, but the honoring God business. More importantly, the point is to remind us that our decision about ministry outreach should be grounded in God's priorities, not strategic, tactical notions about church growth.

No Future In Seniors?

Sadly, I suspect one of the reasons there is such little interest in outreach to seniors is that conventional wisdom suggests that there's just no "future" in it, and from a *human* wisdom perspective, such reasoning might seem valid. In a youth-focused culture, what sense does it make for a church intent upon "growing" to focus outreach efforts and resources on older people "past their prime," with limited energy, and on fixed incomes? We probably all know of churches that have lost their young people, slowly dwindled down, and who have been forced to either close their doors or to eventually merge with another congregation before being forced "out of business." From a conventional wisdom perspective, focusing outreach efforts on seniors sounds like a recipe for disaster for church growth. However, honoring God's priorities is never a recipe for disaster.

Parental And Church Priorities

For those who may still be recovering from the previous "shocking" and politically incorrect statement (i.e. God doesn't need youth ministry to preserve the future of the church) - fasten your seatbelts for another one. Where do we get the notion that youth ministry should be a high priority of the church? Listen carefully to what *was* said and was *not* said - nor implied. What was neither said nor implied was that God doesn't highly value youth. What was neither said nor implied was that children are not a high priority to God. What was asked was where did we get the notion that youth ministry should be a high priority of the *church*. Is the high priority that churches place on youth ministry really from God or from *ourselves*?

The decision to make youth ministry such a high priority ministry of the church is far more subjective and arbitrary or strategic and tactical than it is God ordained. I'm not speaking from a "right" and "wrong" perspective here, but I am challenging churches and church leaders to re-think what is usually just presumed to be "gospel." For those who may react defensively at such a challenge and may feel compelled to justify the high priority placed on youth ministry by churches, allow me to conceding the high priority value and importance of ministry with youth. Any such defensive reaction completely misses the point. I'm all in favor of youth ministry being a high priority ministry of churches. I'm just saying there is as much justification for having a high priority for seniors ministry as there is for having a high priority for youth. In fact, it would seem there is *more* justification. I know of nowhere in scripture where God specifically made youth ministry a high priority of the *church*. I do, however, know of a place in scripture where the *church* readily recognized seniors ministry as one of its highest priorities.

Seniors Were A High Priority Of The Early Church

In Acts 6, it came to the attention of the apostles that some seniors (the Grecian widows) were being treated as a low priority. What's most fascinating and instructive about this text is not *what* the apostles did about it but *how* they responded when this negligence was called to their attention. The text says, "*So the Twelve gathered all the disciples together.*" What an amazing response! Not only did the entire apostleship stop what they were doing and give this their *undivided attention*, but they were even compelled to immediately bring it to the full attention of the *entire congregation*. What's so striking about their response is that the apostles had already solemnly resolved among themselves not to become distracted with anything other than "*the ministry of the word of God*" (Act 6:2). Their willingness – even their *eagerness* to make an exception to their holy resolve for the cause of these neglected senior widows is an incredible testimony to the importance they placed on seniors ministry. By this time, gaining the entire church's undivided attention was no small matter since the Jerusalem church now consisted of at least 5,000 members. Seniors were apparently immediately recognized by the apostles as such a high priority of God's that all twelve apostles essentially said, *"Time out!"* - *"Stop the presses!"* - *"Hold everything!"*

Do the widows mentioned in Acts 6 really illustrate how one of the high priorities of the early church was a *seniors* ministry program? Absolutely! Although there is nothing in the text that reveals their exact age, these widows were certainly far more likely to be *seniors* than younger women. In additional to just using common sense, it is reasonable to conclude that these widows were *senior* widows by looking into both the past and the future. Although these women were *Grecian* widows, they were nevertheless Jews and members of the early Jerusalem *Jewish* church. Since the days of Moses, God's people were more than familiar with how a *young* widow was to become the responsibility of her brother-in-law (Deut. 25). In fact, some legalistic Pharisees once tried to ensnare Jesus in an elaborate hypothetical test about this very issue addressed in the Law of Moses (Mt. 22).

However, more significantly than looking back, perhaps we should "fast forward" to instructions given to the young evangelist Timothy. In his first letter to Timothy (1 Tim. 5), the Apostle Paul makes a clear distinction between younger and older widows when determining which widows should receive special time, attention, and resources from the church. Paul presumed that younger widows would have the option to marry again, whereas older widows, as the King James Version says, would be *"widows indeed"* or truly destitute and in need of some assistance. Unless we are prepared to accuse the Almighty (who claims to be *"the same yesterday, today, and tomorrow"*) of flip-flopping on the issue, we can confidently surmise that when the Spirit guided the Apostles in Acts 6 to formally establish a ministry program for these Grecian widows that they were actually establishing a *seniors* ministry program for older widows.

Apparently, the Apostles understood that ministering to the needs of these senior widows deserved and required not only their undivided attention, but also deserved and required the entire congregation's undivided attention to determine an appropriate course of action. With everything else on their plate, how easily the apostles could have hastily placed the needs of these seniors at the bottom of their "to do" list – or at least somewhere in the middle, but certainly not at the very top of the list. How easily they could have pawned the problem off on one of the "less prominent" apostles and said, *"Hey Thaddaeus, go see what the commotion is all about and take care of it as quickly as possible. Then, get back here immediately so we can continue taking care of the more important matters of the church."* Instead, everything - and I mean *everything* - came to a screeching halt until they had devised a way to more effectively address the unmet needs of these seniors.

That devised way involved far more than scrounging up a few reluctant, half-hearted, half-qualified volunteers to make some minimal, obligatory effort to merely appease some "bellyachers" among them. Rather, it included commissioning the very *best* among them for leading the effort. The Apostles had readily recognized the importance of making more than some minimal effort with seniors. Instead of reserving the most talented and qualified among them for other, "more important" ministry causes, they sought out and devoted the cream of the crop among them who were *"full of faith and of the Holy Spirit."* They sought and selected such specially qualified men for (of all things) ... seniors ministry! When so little emphasis is placed on seniors ministry today, how ironic it is that this was one of the earliest and most highly valued ministries of the Jerusalem church.

The apostles readily recognized the importance of ministering to the needs of these seniors. They didn't need to be talked, coerced, or guilt-tripped into it. Judging from the reaction of the church, the entire congregation spontaneously shared this high priority attitude because verse five says the commitment to begin more adequately addressing the needs of these seniors *"pleased the whole multitude."* The power and significance of these eight words (*"so the twelve gathered all the disciples together"*) may be tragically lost on those of us preoccupied with other priorities, but for those who are committed to making this priority of God's their own, the response of the apostles is stunningly remarkable. It speaks volumes.

What explains such a dramatic shift in priorities away from seniors since the days of the Jerusalem church? There may be multiple reasons but one of them is the contemporary notion that the church simply has a greater responsibility toward youth than seniors. The reasoning is that whereas seniors are grown adults, youth are still under-age and dependent. It is further rationalized that the primary responsibility of meeting the needs of aging parents should fall upon their adult children. I'd be the first to freely acknowledge the dependency of youth upon others for their ministry needs, and that adults, as a general rule, are more accountable for their own ministry needs than are youth. I'd likewise be the first to eagerly encourage and commend churches about making youth ministry a high priority. Furthermore, I'd be the first to acknowledge that adult children of aging parents are the ones *primarily* responsible for meeting the needs of their senior parents.

However (and this is a huge however), the parents of youth are no less the *primary* responsibility of their young children than are the adult children of their aging parents. The church is primarily responsible for neither. Rather, the primary responsibility for caregiving falls upon the *families* of those young children, teens, and aging parents. How, then, can we on the one hand justify youth ministry as a

105

high priority of the *church* while on the other hand presume that the primary responsibility of seniors is not the church but individual families?

We seemingly have no reservations whatsoever with enthusiastically providing exceptional ministry programs to assist younger parents with the primarily *parental* responsibility of *"training up a child in the way that he should go"* (Prov. 22:6) or augmenting the primarily *parental* responsibility to *"bring up children in the nurture and admonition of the Lord"* as mentioned in scripture (Eph. 6:4). However, when it comes to providing equally exceptional ministry programs to assist adult children of aging parents to *"honor your father and mother,"* where is the equitable church ministry response? Perhaps a more significant question is why isn't it there? What's the difference?

In all honesty, is not the different way we justify a high priority for youth ministry and a low priority for seniors inconsistent reasoning? It is not God but the personal preferences of a youth-focused culture that has so convincingly persuaded us to make youth ministry such a high priority ministry of the church. In fact, as has just been discussed, one of the first high priority ministry efforts of the early church was, ironically, seniors. We may be living under the illusion that other ministry efforts are more important than seniors, but nothing will change the *fact* that seniors have been and continue to be one of God's explicitly declared highest priorities since the days of Moses – and was among the first high priorities of the early church.

Old Dogs and New Tricks

I suspect another reason why, when we think about outreach, we don't think much about seniors is because of the fundamentally flawed notion that seniors are simply too "set in their ways" to make much difference anyway. What this implies is that seniors ministry has too little of an exciting and tangible outcome, with too little sensational and verifiable results. Seniors, as a group, have been unfairly saddled with the reputation of being old dogs that can't be taught new tricks. Sadly, there is something fundamentally wrong with this attitude. Where are the scientific studies that verify such an allegation about seniors? Such perceptions are rooted more in anecdotal than scientific evidence.

Ironically, this "old dog/new trick" axiom isn't supported by the facts – even when applied to the tendencies of dogs, much less when discussing the inclinations of seniors. Experts in the field of animal behavior insist that *"with a little ingenuity and perseverance, just about any old dog can do new tricks."* This comes from such experts as Victoria Wells, manager of shelter behavior and training at the ASPCA in New York City, who also appears on Animal Planet's *Animal Precinct*. It also comes from such experts as Trish King, director of animal behavior and training at the Marin, California Humane Society and author of *Parenting Your Dog*.

Beyond the "old dog/new tricks" myth, studies have been conducted on how receptive *seniors* are to change that offer some rather surprising results, according to Abilene Christian University's gerontology department. The old dog/new tricks myth was "blown to smithereens." Ironically, what was discovered was that seniors were actually as open to change as any other age group when as much time, energy, and effort were invested in them as is typically devoted to other generations. Whatever *seemingly* greater propensity for resistance to change that might be generally observed among and attributed to seniors could be directly traced to the disproportionately lesser amount of time spent working closely with them than with younger generations. The clear implication of these studies is that if churches and church leaders began making as much of an effort with seniors as they routinely make with youth, they could expect similar results.

Honest Comparisons

Any *honest* comparison between the potential "results" in ministry with seniors and that of youth would require first investing as much time, attention, and resources with seniors as is routinely given to youth. If we spent as little time, attention, and resources on youth ministry as we do on seniors ministry, we just might find ourselves thinking that "you can't teach a *young* dog new tricks." In fact, don't we see evidence of this with "inner city" families where children are often raised without the benefit of the time, attention, and resources that youth need and deserve? Don't we see evidence of this when an inner city child's mother may be hooked on drugs or at least overwhelmed with life and engulfed in poverty to the point that she can't be the mother she needs to be, and the father may not even be present?

The well-known fact is that such urban social issues stubbornly propagate and perpetuate from generation to generation in a seemingly never-ending and hopeless cycle … until someone begins to invest the time, attention, and resources required to have any meaningful impact. Consequently we have developed government programs to address such poverty issues. More significantly, churches have developed inner city ministry efforts to address moral and spiritual issues. Without the time, attention, and resources that churches and church leaders are willing to give to the inner city, many children in such a situation can certainly appear unable and unwilling to break the "incorrigible" cycle. They appear to be "*young dogs you can't teach new tricks.*" It is when government programs, church ministries, and other philanthropic efforts abandon a "lost cause" mentality about the inner city that we can realistically hope to enact change in the hearts and lives of such inner city children.

The Adaptability Of Seniors

Contrary to conventional "wisdom," today's seniors have actually shown great adaptability and resiliency to change. We're told that there have been more changes in the world (especially in the fields of science, technology, and inventions) in the last 100 years than since the world began. Think of how drastically different the world is today than when today's seniors were children, teenagers, or young adults. Then think about how well so many seniors have not only adapted to but welcomed many of these changes. They've gone from riding in horse-driven buggies to driving automobiles at 70 miles per hour in rush hour traffic. They've gone from never venturing far from home to taking commercial airline flights across the country and the world. They've gone from wood burning cook stoves to microwave ovens. They've gone from handwritten letters, mail boxes, and the postal service to firing up the computer and sending emails instantly over the internet. They've gone from hand-cranked, landline phones to cellular service.

Over and over again, seniors have demonstrated an amazing willingness, as well as an ability, to adjust, adapt, and welcome change. Characterizing them as little more than "old dogs" too set in their ways to learn new things is demeaning and simply doesn't square with the facts. Admittedly, I've met and known stubborn seniors who are set in their ways. I've also met and known plenty from younger generations who were just as stubbornly set in their ways. Seniors have hardly "cornered the market" on unyielding closed-mindedness. Resistance to change is not an issue of chronology but attitude and relationship.

It's Not About Outcomes but Outreach

The "bottom line" of any ministry effort really shouldn't be about outcomes but outreach. However, in the business world and even within the church we want outcomes. We want results. We crave some tangible, verifiable way (preferably numbers) to measure our "success." Outcomes are good, as are tangible, verifiable means of measuring efforts – but they're not always reliable criteria. Furthermore, they may perhaps never be the most important thing, especially when it comes to ministry efforts and outreach. Not everything in life is about achieving desired outcomes or required results. Sometimes life is about doing the right thing simply because it's the right thing to do. If ministering to the needs of seniors in an exceptional way is the right thing to do, then that alone should be sufficient reason for doing seniors ministry exceptionally – regardless of outcomes.

When God set the boundaries for Adam and Eve in the Garden of Eden to eat anything they wanted except from the tree of the knowledge of good and evil, there was certainly a desired outcome. Regardless of the desired outcome, however, they also had an obligation and responsibility to simply honor God's instructions. They were likewise obliged to honor Him regardless of consequences. God always has good reasons (desired outcomes) for the instructions He has given. Those who are wise enough to follow His instructions will enjoy and experience His desired outcomes. However, honoring God's will is not just about achieving His outcomes.

It's Not About Outcomes But Faithfulness

Additionally, when it comes to ministry, Paul spoke of how our "job" is to simply *plant* and *water*, while leaving the *increase* up to God (1 Cor. 3:6). When Jesus issued the Great Commission, He didn't say, "*Achieve XYZ number of conversions per week, month, or year.*" Rather, He commissioned believers to simply encourage others to become fellow students of Christ (Mt. 28). When the Corinthian believers became more focused on the "results" of various church leaders than upon simply living and spreading the good news, Paul wanted nothing to do with it (1 Cor. 1). It's not about "*measuring ourselves*" by faulty standards (2 Cor. 10:12).

Results can be useful in helping confirm our ministry efforts and can provide encouragement, but God has never commanded us to "get results." Hear that again! God has never demanded specific outcomes from our ministry efforts – never! He has told us to bear fruit, but He has never required us to meet "quotas." When we make an effort, we *will* bear fruit, but God doesn't require results that are necessarily quantifiable by human standards and measurements. We have superimposed that burden upon ourselves. God has asked for our best effort. He has also asked for our faithfulness to His cause. However, He has never required an outcome because results are not up to us, but to Him. Even the man who had been given one talent and failed to expand his master's investment was not guilty of failed outcomes and results as much as he was guilty of failing to even make an *effort* because of his "wicked and slothful" misperceptions of his master (Mt. 25).

It's Not End Results But Process

As far as our ministry efforts go, God is far more interested in the *process* than the end results. Bring a little bit of fish and a few loaves of bread to the table and God can take care of the resulting outcome. Our commission is not to get results or even focus on outcomes but to simply be faithful to His calling. So when we plan, pursue, and evaluate ministry efforts on the basis of results, we're operating with a faulty premise. Our ministry efforts are about simple obedience and faithfulness, regardless of results. Consequently, the driving force behind our ministry efforts with seniors should be simple obedience and faithfulness to this high priority of God's.

No Senior Left Behind

In recent years, our government initiated a school program policy called, "No Child Left Behind." This program recognized that even in as great a nation as ours, some children in our education system were still "falling through the cracks." Despite certified teachers and carefully planned curriculums as well as federal, state, and local oversight, children were still "left behind." Similarly, one branch of our military service, the Marines, has long had a similar "no soldier left behind" on the battlefield policy and perspective. We need to develop a "no *seniors* left behind" attitude about seniors on the battlefield of life. Even in an educational system where students are surrounded by certified teachers and carefully planned curriculum, children can still be left behind in the classroom unless there is a *conscious* desire with an *intentional* plan to reach out to them. Even within a well trained military where soldiers are fully armed and equipped, soldiers can be left behind on the battlefield unless there is a *conscious* desire with an *intentional* plan to reach out to them. Similarly, even within a community of servant-hearted believers, seniors can be left behind unless there is a *conscious* desire with an *intentional* plan to reach out to them.

To Do And To Teach

Outreach to and with seniors, as with any group, best begins with meeting needs effectively and sufficiently. This was one of the distinct characteristics of Jesus' ministry efforts. He routinely saw a need, filled it … and *then* taught the ones He had served. In fact, this was so characteristic of His ministry that when penning the book of Acts, Luke described the ministry of Jesus as one that was an account of "*all that Jesus began both to do and to teach*" (Act 1:1). Why did the author of Acts say "*do and teach*" instead of "*teach and do?*" Perhaps there was no intended significance, but I suspect the order of those two action words were intentional. Ironically, even though Jesus was far more concerned about the *spiritual* needs of those He healed than He was with their *physical* needs, His outreach often began with meeting physical needs before addressing spiritual needs. This is not to say that ministry outreach must always begin with meeting physical needs. It is simply to say that Jesus' "do and teach" approach to ministry usually makes for more effective ministry outreach, whether with seniors or any other age group. Most people, as the old saying goes, "*simply don't care how much we know until they know how much we care.*" Meeting the ministry needs of seniors plays a significant role in providing exceptional ministry with seniors.

Unintended Consequences

However, we must be mindful during the process of addressing and meeting the ministry needs of seniors that we avoid causing or encouraging the unintended consequence of creating dependency. As important as it is to *meet* needs, it's equally important that we don't *cause* unnecessary dependency. Remember – one of the fundamental ministry needs of seniors is providing assistance *when lacking ability*. Although we shouldn't allow a mere *potential* for causing "unintended consequences" to dampen our outreach efforts to meet the needs of seniors, we should be mindfully aware of that possibility and proceed accordingly.

Backfire

To illustrate how easily our well-intended efforts to meet needs can "backfire" in the form of dependency, look at how this has happened to so many government assistance programs over and over again. One of the more unfortunate shortcomings of most governmental welfare programs is that they have all too often caused dependency on the part of the very ones whom the program was intended to actually aid. All too often, these well-intended programs not only cause dependency but exacerbate the very problem they are intended to help. For example, all the welfare efforts over the last 40-50 years have resulted in an *increase* in the number of poor people (nearly 15 million on welfare and a tripling in the percentage of children on welfare).

This increase in dependency has occurred despite the numerous and often redundant federal aid programs that have, in good faith, been created - programs such as the Aid to Families with Dependent Children Program, the Women-Infant-Children Program (WIC), the Commodity Supplemental Food Program, the School Lunch Program, the School Breakfast Program, the School Milk Program, the Child and Adult Care Food Program, the Summer Feeding Program, the Nutrition Program for the Elderly, the Needy Family Program, the Emergency Food Assistance Program, and on and on. The Food Stamps Program alone is a $33 billion effort. Since the 1960's, our government has spent 6.6 trillion dollars on welfare efforts to end poverty.

Unnecessary Dependency

These well-intended efforts have been at least as successful in creating greater dependency upon a growing number of people as they have been actually meeting the needs of recipients in such a way that helps lift them out of poverty. However, this should come as no surprise because any time you do for another what they can do for themselves, you create an ideal environment for establishing unnecessary dependency ... and often an even greater dependency. Such efforts are more counterproductive than helpful. Good intentions on our part simply are not good enough ... if we're more interested in genuinely *helping* others than we are in merely feeling good about ourselves for trying to help others.

Consider all the unintended consequences that occur in our welfare program efforts. One example can be seen when a single-parent mother has a child out of wedlock, gets on welfare, and proceeds to have additional children out of wedlock in order to generate additional welfare income for herself. Another example can be seen when out-of-work but able-bodied welfare recipients actually avoid getting a job because they'd rather live off welfare (even at a level of subsistence) than work for a living. It demonstrates why, when scripture addresses one's inclination toward idleness, even God's attitude is, *"If someone is unwilling to work, don't allow him to freeload off your good will"* (2 Thes. 3:10). Un*able* is one thing but un*willing* is quite another.

Finding Needs ... or Creating Needs

When it comes to meeting the ministry needs of seniors, we must likewise be mindful that we are meeting needs where assistance is actually needed – and not created. Otherwise, such ministry efforts will create a dependency class among seniors, much like government welfare has created a dependency class among those whom it was intended to help lift out of poverty. This is not at all to say that we should have anything other than an unrestrained eagerness to meet the ministry needs of seniors. It's just to say that our ministry efforts with seniors shouldn't fall into the same trap that our government welfare efforts have fallen into when trying to do a good thing.

Seniors, especially aging seniors, need to be encouraged to remain as active and independent as possible for as long as possible. We do them no favors to do for them (on a regular basis) what they can do for themselves. Offering occasional help simply as a surprise treat, an expression of love, or to offer a well deserved break would be a wonderful idea. Parents of young children, for example, may not need assistance with their child on a *regular* basis, but a next door neighborhood friend occasionally babysitting their neighbor's child for an evening while the parents go out for a meal and a movie together is a wonderful idea. Such parents aren't "lacking the ability" to care for their child, but having an occasional break from the responsibility is a good thing. However, it would be an entirely different matter if that neighborhood friend, regardless of how well-intended, were to offer to completely take over all or even most responsibilities for raising that child when that child's parents are fully capable of doing it themselves.

My mother, for example, still lives in the same house in which I grew up. Although she has several health conditions for which she takes medication, she is a very active lady for her age. She is able to drive herself to the grocery store, the post office, the bank, the mall, and to church. She does her own laundry. In fact, even though she has both a washer and dryer, she prefers to hang her clothes out on the backyard clothesline when the weather allows. She works in her yard sweeping both the sidewalk and the driveway, while also raking and bagging leaves during the fall. Twice a week she wheels the large garbage container out to the edge of the street. She is still very able to do many things.

As well-intended as the ministry effort might be, it would be a mistake for a seniors ministry program in her home church to begin meeting these needs for her on a regular basis while she still has the ability to do them for herself. To do them on an occasional basis would be an entirely different matter. It would be marvelous for a church's ministry efforts with seniors to include *occasionally* doing such yard work for my mother just as an expression of love, even though she still has the ability to do it herself. However, for a church's seniors ministry program to completely assume those tasks for her (or for any other capable seniors) in the name of an exceptional seniors ministry program would be both unnecessary (as long as she can do them herself) and actually contrary to her best interest.

On the other hand, there are numerous things my mother is no longer able to do for herself that would be exactly the kind of needs a seniors ministry program could and should be addressing for seniors on a regular basis. For example, she cannot change a ceiling light bulb in the kitchen, when it goes out. Her equilibrium will no longer permit her to safely stand on a stool and look upwards. Likewise, she has neither the strength nor the stamina to mow her beautiful yard or to move large tree limbs that occasionally break and fall into the yard. Presently she is financially able to pay someone in the neighborhood to do these things for her. However, the time may come when she no longer has such an option.

An exceptional seniors ministry program includes meeting the needs of seniors who are lacking the ability to meet those needs themselves. It recognizes that efforts must be proactive in finding and discovering such unmet needs of seniors. Furthermore, it understands that the best way to discover the unmet ministry needs of seniors is by relying upon personal, intergenerational relationships (i.e. a relational assessment) that are intentionally formed with seniors, rather than by utilizing some impersonal check-list survey. However, exceptional seniors ministry also understands the difference between *discovering* needs and unintentionally *creating* them.

Healthy Self-Reliance or Unhealthy Dependency
How we go about meeting the needs of others can spell the difference between finding needs and creating them. This can be the difference between encouraging a healthy self-reliance and causing an unhealthy dependency. When an impersonal government with an impersonal program impersonally establishes impersonal criteria for impersonal recipients, resources are spent that could and should have been spent elsewhere more wisely. Providing welfare for an able-bodied single mom when it's merely more *convenient* for her to remain perpetually on the welfare roll is not in her best interest. Helping her in such a way that actually gives her a *dis*incentive to become self-supporting is neither in the best interest of that recipient, nor is it in the best interest of other recipients who genuinely *are* unable to meet their own needs.

Using Limited Resources Wisely
This is why a *relational* assessment of needs is so much more effective (and accurate) than an impersonal survey. A relational approach to assessing the needs of seniors can more effectively distinguish between meeting authentic needs and providing dependency-causing service. If, for example, a seniors ministry program determined to begin mowing the yards for *all* the seniors in the congregation, invariably there would be some who might enjoy or appreciate the help but who don't *need* the help. There is certainly nothing "wrong" with mowing yards for seniors who are able to take care of their own yards, but it can encourage dependency. It also depletes limited resources unnecessarily.

A far better approach would be to target only the yards of seniors who, through a relational assessment of ministry needs, were discovered to be unable to care for their

113

own yards. This would be the most effective and efficient use of limited resources. It would also encourage rather than discourage active ministry volunteers. Few things discourage volunteers more from either becoming or remaining involved with a cause than doing a task that is unnecessary. Most people, even service-minded and service-hearted believers, simply have better things to do with their time than spend it on activities they know are largely unnecessary. One of the quickest ways to derail a seniors ministry program is to ask volunteers to begin providing unnecessary services.

A Place To Begin Outreach

An obvious place to begin reaching the unmet ministry needs of seniors is with the seniors within your own home congregation. This is a good place to begin, but it is not the place to end. After carefully and comprehensively identifying as well as meeting their ministry needs (preferably through a relationship assessment), outreach could and should continually, outwardly expand by including, for example, neighbors or acquaintances of any and all members of the congregation. If, for example, a young couple who are members of a church live next door to an aging senior who may need help, that young couple certainly could and should reach out to that senior themselves. This situation could, however, also present an outreach opportunity for the church's seniors ministry program if the needs were more than that couple could handle alone.

A Place To Continue Outreach

Another place of outreach to seniors is at any of the senior living facilities within the community and throughout the city. As was briefly mentioned in chapter three but will be discussed in greater depth in chapter nine, I have visited seniors in senior living facilities for years and found them to be a tremendous opportunity for ministry outreach. I have witnessed first-hand how seniors can receive state-of-the-art *physical* care in even the most luxurious facility in the city and still not have their *spiritual* needs addressed. Senior living facilities are simply not intended to address *spiritual* needs. Most do have an activities director who provides entertaining and social opportunities. Some facilities even welcome churches to provide in-house "church services" for residents who are interested.

Providing Sunday afternoon services and/or mid-week devotionals are excellent beginnings for addressing more than the physical, medical, and housing needs of such seniors living in a community environment ... but only beginnings. This should be considered no more sufficient for adequately meeting the spiritual needs of seniors than would Sunday services be considered sufficient for adequately meeting the needs of children and teens or young and middle-age adults. They need to be offered more spiritual nourishment and encouragement than that, as do seniors at a senior living community. We seem to readily understand this when it comes to younger generations, which is why so much time, attention, and resources are devoted to them in ministry programs, activities, and outreach. However, we seemingly either fail to ... or refuse to understand it when it comes to seniors.

In principle, providing such seniors additional spiritual nourishment beyond "in-house" church services is accomplished the same way it is provided for younger generations. The specifics may be different but the principle is the same. It requires additional time, effort, and activities. The possibilities are only as limited as our imagination and our commitment to exceptional seniors ministry. Additional efforts can include visiting individual residents regularly at *other* times for the purpose of building friendships and fellowship. Activities could include such things as studying scripture, praying, reading a novel together, discussing family backgrounds or current events, helping them write a memoirs book for their family, knitting gifts for the homeless, writing notes of encouragement to others, taking a walk, playing table games, and giving them a manicure. Additional efforts can also include taking them on periodic outings. Activities can include such things as having them into your home for tea or a family meal, including them in a bridge club meeting, taking them out to eat, going to a movie, visiting the art center, taking them on a scenic drive in the country or to their old neighborhood, making a trip to the supermarket or department store, and treating them at the local ice cream shop.

Using The Youth Ministry Blueprint

Exactly what those age-specific service opportunities could be is something that must be determined by each church's seniors ministry program for their specific seniors. Whatever those age-specific opportunities are, and however they are most effectively implemented, they can be determined the same way we determine age-specific successful ministry efforts for youth or any other ages (via interests, capabilities, giftedness, timing, importance, potential, etc.). Because churches are generally doing such an exemplary job with their youth ministry program, both in terms of meeting age-specific needs, as well as providing age-specific service opportunities, it would be wise to simply apply some of the same principle components used in today's exceptional youth ministry programs as a "blueprint" for building an equally exceptional *seniors* ministry program.

Fully Focused Ministry Leader

One of the most crucial components of an exceptionally effective youth ministry program for meeting age-specific needs and providing age-specific service opportunities for youth is having someone to lead the ministry program with a fully focused, full-time effort. Does having a seniors ministry program absolutely require having someone working at it full time? ... No, not any more than having a youth ministry program requires having a full-time youth minister. However, having an *exceptional* seniors ministry program, like having an exceptional youth ministry program, requires someone's full-time attention – and not just anyone's full-time attention.

115

Any of today's *exceptional* youth ministry programs requires a special individual to lead the effort – qualified in terms of skills, experience, and passion for the ministry. Exceptional youth ministry programs don't become exceptional by relying upon some mediocre, loosely organized effort led by half-focused volunteers ... and neither can exceptional seniors ministry programs. We realize that if we want an exceptional youth ministry program for our youth, we need an exceptional individual to lead that full-time effort in a very skilled and energetic way. It requires someone who is creative and innovative as well as someone who is given an opportunity to focus his full-time attention on it. *Exceptional* youth ministry necessitates providing someone with the necessary time, attention, and resources needed for developing an exceptional youth ministry program.

Why should we think it would take anything less to have an exceptional *seniors* ministry program? As the old saying goes, "*You get what you pay for*" most of the time. We're willing to do whatever it requires for developing an exceptional youth ministry program because we *seriously* care for our youth. If it takes someone's full-time attention, so be it. If it takes finding the best possible ministry leader, so be it. If we're not willing to do the same for a seniors ministry program, what does that say about how much we care for seniors and their ministry needs?

Leadership Endorsement

A second crucial component of a youth ministry program that meets age-specific needs and provides age-specific service opportunities in an exceptional way is having the full and enthusiastic endorsement of the church leadership. It's not enough to simply *have* a seniors ministry program or even create a full-time staff position for a highly qualified individual. That very effort, and the one leading that effort, must have the enthusiastic endorsement of the church's leadership. This usually occurs naturally when it comes to youth ministry, but a more intentional and deliberate effort may be required by church leaders when it involves showing their enthusiastic public support for seniors ministry. I'm not talking about "faking it" but simply ensuring that the seniors ministry program is as publicly praised, heavily highlighted, and enthusiastically endorsed as is the youth ministry program.

An exceptional seniors ministry program needs and requires as much "corporate" prominence as any other exceptional ministry effort of the church. Leaders must be continually affirming the need for, as well as the value, importance, and urgency of seniors ministry to help generate interest and involvement from members. Just like an exceptional teen or children ministry program cannot become exceptional without the help of committed, involved, and enthusiastic volunteers, an exceptional seniors ministry program cannot become exceptional by the efforts of only one or a few volunteers. Just as a full-time youth minister wisely relies upon the involvement of others to develop a creative and innovative program that can be implemented in an exceptional way, a full-time seniors minister must also rely upon the involvement of others for developing and implementing an exceptional seniors ministry program. Seniors ministry is no more about merely "hiring someone to go visit the old folks" than youth ministry is about merely hiring someone to play video games with teens. There is so much more involved in developing an exceptional seniors ministry program. It requires the whole-hearted support of the church's leadership.

Creative And Innovative Thinking

A third crucial component of a youth ministry program that meets age-specific needs and provides age-specific service opportunities in an exceptional way is being creative and innovative, as has been touched upon previously. There's a reason ministry with today's youth doesn't look like it did 30 years ago ... or even ten years ago. This necessity for continual creativity and innovation is as true in the world of ministry as it is in the business world. There is a reason why the marketing departments of corporations and industries are constantly changing and adapting how they reach and service their customers as time passes and things change.

For example, what entrepreneurial enterprise would attract or keep customers today if all it was offering was antiquated telegraph communication service? How effective would a company be today that was still (only) providing sales and service for Commodore 64 computers (for those who may not know or remember, they were one of the original PC's made available to the public many years ago)? What patient would be interested in going to a physician who was still using medical procedures from the medieval ages? Even though the telegraph was "cutting edge" in its time, the Commodore 64 served its customers well at the dawn of the PC age, and physicians from the medieval age offered "state-of-the-art" care in their time, these are neither sufficient nor effective in today's world. Churches can no more adequately meet the needs of today's seniors without utilizing continual creativity and innovation in their ministry efforts than can the business world satisfactorily meet the needs of customers by providing yesterday's solutions.

The need for change is no poor reflection upon any previous efforts with seniors ministry anymore than it is a poor reflection upon any of our previous efforts with youth. In fact, today's more creative and innovative efforts with youth are built upon the foundation of preceding efforts. Similarly, the need for more creative and innovative efforts with seniors can and will be built upon the foundation of previous efforts that have been made with seniors. Changes in *how* we do ministry no more slight previous foundational efforts than does the Law of Christ slight the Law of Moses.

Today's exceptional youth ministry programs have, in principle, provided an ideal blueprint for exceptional ministry in general. Ironically, they have pioneered the way for more effective seniors ministry. If we don't share God's *priority* for seniors, all we have to do is continue doing what is already being done. If, however, we

117

recognize the importance of seniors and seniors ministry as much as we do that of youth and youth ministry, there is no need to "reinvent the wheel." Exceptional youth ministry programs have already shown the way. The best way to help maintain and ensure an exceptional youth ministry program is to utilize the crucial components upon which exceptional youth ministry programs have been built. And the best way to help ensure an exceptional *seniors* ministry program is to utilize the same crucial components that have made contemporary youth ministry programs so effective. Like a solid three-legged stool, a seniors ministry program that consists of these crucial components (fully focused leadership for the ministry effort, the church leadership's public and enthusiastic endorsement, and creative innovation) can be built upon a solid foundation for exceptional ministry with seniors.

CHAPTER EIGHT
Pastures Are Way Overrated!
(*served to serve*)

When thinking about seniors ministry, many think about "taking care of" seniors. Caregiving (which will be discussed in chapter ten) is certainly a significant part of seniors ministry, but it's only *part* of the story. Seniors ministry is as much about *seniors serving* as it is about *serving seniors*. It's as big of a mistake to presume that seniors ministry is all or even mostly about serving seniors as it would be to presume that youth ministry is all or mostly about serving teens to the virtual exclusion of encouraging and empowering teens to learn to serve.

Today's Seniors Want To Serve
Ministry with seniors is about meeting their *ministry needs*, while also utilizing their giftedness for *ministry opportunities to serve*. For *older* seniors, whose frailty may be more advanced, the appropriate focus might be more upon their ministry *needs*. However, research indicates that today's seniors who are still relatively healthy see their senior years more as a lifestyle change and a new opportunity than as the conclusion of a career or the end of a meaningful life. According to AARP surveys, nearly 70 percent expect to continue working well into their "retirement" years. Only 17 percent want a "typical" retirement. This presents a tremendous opportunity for churches ... if they prepare sufficiently ahead of time!

However, these seniors are reportedly turning to retirement coaches, retirement self-help groups, and retirement retreats (i.e. instead of to churches). They're turning *elsewhere* for inspiration and ideas for opportunities about how they'll focus their time, energy, and resources during their senior years. They're turning elsewhere so much so that it is literally creating an entire "silver industry," according to Harry Moody, director of academic affairs for AARP. In fact, according to recent research at civicventures.org by the non-profit MetLife Foundation and San Francisco Civic Ventures, a trend seems to be developing among seniors that some have identified as "encore careers" where millions of boomer seniors are either quitting their old jobs or coming out of retirement to pursue new careers that not only give them personal meaning but also contribute to society.

Is it any wonder such seniors are not looking to churches for serving opportunities when seniors ministry is apparently valued so little and is given such an insignificant amount of time, attention, and resources? We have a special opportunity to remedy this unfortunate consequence of our neglect. IF our "lamps of preparation" for seniors ministry are filled and trimmed with innovative programs, adequate budgets, and visionary leadership for ministry with today's seniors, such seniors will have a reason to turn to churches for possible service opportunities. This is why a giftedness assessment, as discussed in chapter six, is important. Such assessments need to be done as early as possible with participating seniors once churches commit to developing an exceptional seniors ministry program. However, as essential as it is for seniors to know how God has gifted them to serve, it's equally essential for churches and church leaders to ensure that they help provide opportunities for seniors to utilize their God-giftedness.

Age-Specific Service Opportunities

Many opportunities can be found by simply helping seniors "plug in" to the various ministry programs and efforts that already exist within a congregation. However, we should be eager to also provide *age-specific* opportunities for seniors to exercise their giftedness when such opportunities don't already exist. These additional service opportunities should be designed around their unique abilities, interests, and limitations. Some might question the need for establishing special, additional opportunities merely for the purpose of providing more age-specific opportunities for seniors to serve. However, the irony is that we have already been creating special, additional, age-specific opportunities routinely ... for younger generations.

Sometimes, an age-specific opportunity we provide for teens may take the form of a group missionary trip structured especially for youth. Other times, it may take the form of a summer work/service camp, where teens may spend a week serving the inner city community by painting houses. Whatever forms those additional opportunities may take that are provided, they are age-specific service opportunities structured especially for youth. Why, then, would we even hesitate, much less resist the notion of providing additional age-specific service opportunities for *seniors*? Why the discrepancy, unless we value our seniors less than we value our youth? Seniors will, in some ways, be able to simply "plug in" to already existing service opportunities (just as our youth can), but additional age-specific service opportunities should also be provided for them, just as they are provided for youth.

A homebound senior provides an excellent illustration of the value of providing age-specific service opportunities. A homebound senior, by conventional thinking, would typically be viewed as someone to serve but not one who has anything to offer in the way of serving others. Granted, there are seniors in the extreme stages of failing heath who are no longer in a position to serve, but this is not the case for most

120

seniors. Even homebound seniors can find meaningful places to serve in God's kingdom - with help from an exceptional seniors ministry program that provides and promotes age and situation specific service opportunities. The serving opportunities, however, must be authentic opportunities, not patronizing busy work to merely coddle *"the poor ole soul just to make them feel important."* Such condescension is not only transparent, it's actually uninspiring, demeaning, and even hurtful. If we hold no genuine value in the service opportunity (i.e. we would see little value in doing it ourselves), chances are they won't either.

Prayer Partners Ministry

So what are some age-specific service opportunities that even a homebound or physically limited senior might find personally meaningful in a one-on-one partnership with another believer? What could they do that would be an authentically valuable service opportunity? The most obvious opportunity that comes to mind would be for homebound seniors to become "prayer partners" with the church on behalf of individuals, situations, and circumstances. However, it should be an authentic *partnership* with members of the congregation who are genuinely involved with and seriously committed to such a prayer partner ministry. In fact, the key to such a prayer partner ministry's meaningfulness rests in the authenticity of the partnership. It needs to be a genuinely *mutual* effort between the homebound senior and that senior's prayer partner.

The partnership should go far deeper than merely asking homebound seniors to pray over a prayer list that has been handed to them. It can include such things as praying *together* during regular visits. The partnership can include having the homebound senior's prayer partner always bringing a prayer list of people and things to pray about during each visit. The homebound seniors should be encouraged to come up with their own list, too. Their prayers could focus upon individuals, situations, and circumstances related to both partners' own families and beyond. What and how many items are on the prayer list during each visit is not as important as ensuring that the effort is an authentic partnership. Each prayer partner could have several items to pray about each week, or they could agree to have only one item each to pray about. Another possibility could be to develop the prayer list during the visit while having meaningful conversation and fellowship. The important thing is that the effort be a genuine and authentic *partnership* resulting from a genuine and authentic *relationship*.

Such a prayer partner ministry provides a meaningful ministry opportunity for homebound believers who are interested in serving as "prayer warriors" for the church and on behalf of others. It also provides an opportunity for challenging and equipping the prayer *partners* of seniors who might need to grow in their prayer life. The discipline of authentic prayer can be as challenging and elusive as it is simple. Most believers have much to experientially learn about prayer … not the mechanics of it (picking a time and place to close our eyes or fall on bended knee and clasp our hands as we bow our heads) but the actual "mastering" of prayer.

As simple as prayer seemingly is, the twelve disciples were still baffled by it. Surely one of the most strikingly peculiar and profound requests they ever made of Jesus was "*Teach us to pray*" (Lk. 11:11). Just as it would have been a mistake to presume that the disciples were prayer partner ready with "no assembly required," we should not presume that homebound seniors should simply be handed a prayer list. On some occasions, it might be an opportunity to help homebound seniors grow in their prayer life. On other occasions, however, it might become an opportunity for seasoned senior believers to help their younger prayer partners grow in their prayer life.

An exceptional seniors ministry program will help make this service opportunity meaningful by keeping the prayer requests specific. The prayer requests should be about specific individuals, situations, and circumstances. I'll never forget the "ultimate generic prayer" I actually heard during a Sunday morning assembly many years ago. That dear brother said, "*We pray for those for whom it's our duty to pray*." I could almost see God leaning forward on His throne with a perplexed and confused look on His face cupping his ear and slightly squinting his eyes with concentration as He replied, "*Say what?!?*" Such a generic prayer defies an answer! Such a generic prayer is so vague that it could almost stump the Almighty!

What's the actual point of such a prayer? How in the world would God answer such a prayer? More significantly, what's the point in even saying such a prayer? Although this may be an extreme example of saying prayers rather than praying (talking) to God, shouldn't our prayers be very specific, even if we bathe them, as Jesus did, with a ""*nevertheless not my will but Yours be done*" attitude? Obviously, discretion will be needed in determining what is appropriate to share with others from a prayer list. People and circumstances that should not be disclosed to others should be excluded. However, for prayer on behalf of people and circumstances where confidentiality is not required, sharing such requests with prayer partners would be both appropriate and purposeful.

Exceptional seniors ministry can help make this service opportunity even more meaningful for such homebound seniors and their prayer partners by keeping a running prayer journal. This journal could then be periodically reviewed together as they discussed how God has worked with those mutually prayed for individuals, situations, and circumstances. If homebound seniors are unable to keep their own journal, the prayer partner could help keep one for both of them. For homebound seniors who are able to keep their own prayer journals, perhaps two journals with two different perspectives could be kept and occasionally shared. Just like writing down and tracking personal goals can help offer a greater awareness of and appreciation for those efforts, keeping a prayer journal can help provide a deeper awareness of and appreciation for prayer efforts – and for the working of God in our prayer life. Through such sharing times, prayer partners can experience deeply meaningful fellowship with each other that they would otherwise never experience.

Encouragement Ministry

Another service opportunity that even a homebound or physically limited senior might find personally meaningful and that would be an authentically valuable service opportunity would be an "encouragement ministry." There are countless individuals who could use an "atta boy" and a pat on the back for a job well done. There are too many unsung heroes in the church and in the world, as well as too many thankless tasks that many are faithfully doing daily. Such unsung heroes might include members who volunteer countless hours of service to the church in low profile ways, local citizens who freely donate their time to some small community organization, the custodial staff or groundskeeper of the congregation, or a missionary on the other side of the world. By writing notes and making phone calls or sending emails of encouragement to such individuals, homebound seniors can have an important and powerful ministry.

In the spirit of *"rejoice with those who rejoice"* (Rom. 12:15), those involved in an encouragement ministry can also bless others by simply sharing in the joy of others by making congratulatory calls to parents of newborns or adoptees and to those who have recently been baptized into Christ. What better source for some upbeat words of encouragement to some unappreciated or discouraged soul than from some homebound senior! What better person with whom to mutually rejoice than with a homebound senior who cares enough to take the time to affirm others in their times of joy! What more powerful modeling of faith through encouraging notes and phone calls than from an aging believer whom recipients know face their own limitations and health challenges!

Seniors who have experienced hardships in life such as failing health, the loss of loved ones, or the challenges of living on fixed incomes and yet persevere with a message of encouragement for others (both in word and deed) have credibility that makes their words of encouragement all the more powerful for others to receive. However, an encouragement ministry with homebound seniors (or with any other seniors) would have to be taken as seriously as any other important ministry effort. An exceptional seniors ministry program would need involved volunteers working closely with any seniors interested in becoming encouragers by providing as much assistance as may be needed, both initially and on an ongoing basis. Just as seniors engaged in a prayer partner ministry would need a prayer partner, homebound seniors engaged in an encouragement ministry would need an encouragement partner who could meet with them and provide specific names and circumstances, notecards, stamps, and other helpful materials as needed. More artistically minded or computer-

123

savvy seniors might even help design a line of special occasion cards to mail to others.

Barnabas, The Encourager

The importance and value of being an encourager (i.e. having an "encouragement ministry") should never be underestimated. The Apostle Paul's companion, Barnabas, is a good example. In comparison to Paul, very little is revealed in scripture about Barnabas. He is only briefly introduced in scripture in Acts 4:26 but even then he appears only to provide a context for the story of Ananias and Sapphira. We don't read about him again until Paul finds himself struggling to make a transition from persecutor to proclaimer of Jesus among the Christian Jews (Acts 9:26ff). At this time Barnabas stands in the gap for Paul by encouraging fearful Jewish believers to receive and accept this formerly vicious enemy of the faith.

When doubt and confusion arose over whether the good news was also for Gentiles, the church sent Barnabas to Antioch to investigate. Barnabas served as an ambassador of encouragement (Acts 11:19ff). Barnabas' very name means "son of encouragement." One of the most powerful aspects of Barnabas' ministry was his effort to simply encourage others. In fact, Barnabas was so committed to being an encourager that he and Paul eventually had a serious "falling out" over a young man named John Mark (Acts 15:36f). Paul was adamantly unwilling to include John Mark on another missionary journey because John Mark had apparently abandoned them previously at Pamphylia. Paul had "written him off," but Barnabas, the encourager, never lost sight of John Mark's potential. He was steadfastly committed to encouraging this young man's budding faith.

There was such a sharp contention between Paul and Barnabas over this that the unthinkable occurred. Their seemingly inseparable partnership was not only shaken but dissolved. Paul absolutely refused to include John Mark, while Barnabas was not ready to give up on his young cousin. Time proved Barnabas right. Paul later recognized and acknowledged how Barnabas' determination to continue encouraging John Mark eventually paid off. Even the strong-willed Apostle Paul came to see John Mark as a useful and valuable asset (2 Tim. 4:11, Col. 4:10). We live in a fallen world filled with discouragement and doubt where Satan is doing everything he can to cause overwhelming despair. He tempts many to simply give up. What could be more valuable than to empower homebound seniors to have an "encouragement ministry" that powerfully blesses others? Who but God knows what "John Marks" or "Pauls" a homebound senior with the spirit and character of Barnabas may help through some difficult transition or faith trial on their way to fulfilling their calling from God?

124

Authentic Encouragement

For an encouragement ministry to be an *authentic* service opportunity for seniors, it must be an authentically *mutual* effort. An authentically mutual effort requires more than merely suggesting to seniors that they become "encouragers." It must be pursued in a genuinely authentic way. As with a prayer partner ministry, participating homebound seniors in an encouragement ministry would have to be kept informed and updated enough about the church's activities to feel genuinely connected enough to write personal notes of thanks, appreciation, and commendation for the individual efforts of fellow believers.

Any information shared would, of course, need to be such that could be shared with others for ministry purposes (i.e. not confidential). Recipients of the notes of encouragement don't have to be limited to members of the congregation. By helping such homebound seniors to remain informed about community, state, and national events (as well as church activities), they could also be presented with golden opportunities to send needed notes of thanks and commendation or calls of appreciation to an even wider range of individuals.

Additional Service Opportunities

Additional service opportunities that an exceptional seniors ministry program could help encourage and provide for more than merely homebound seniors are limited only by the imagination of those committed to pursuing seniors ministry as seriously and enthusiastically as other ministries we passionately pursue with continual creativity and innovation. Those service opportunities are best identified by first focusing on the areas of giftedness and interests of each senior member within the congregation. Only then would you proceed with helping them find or create ways to exercise their giftedness in service to others.

Attempting to provide within the pages of this book a generic, one-size-fits-all list of such service opportunities for seniors would be of limited value because the possibilities would be as diverse, unique, and numerous as the giftedness and interests of each senior in every congregation. It would also do churches a disservice for at least a couple of reasons. First, it would deprive them of the process of engaging in their own creative and innovative brainstorming session for discovering and developing their own service opportunities. Second, it would rob them of the opportunity to take more personal ownership of the outcome which is a crucial part of the process. A couple of examples can sufficiently illustrate the principle and stir the imagination.

A senior who is (or was) a Certified Public Account might help older seniors during the tax season with their taxes. However, the odds are high that the last thing such a senior would be interested in doing as his own personal ministry is more accountant work. If this is the case, perhaps he can serve through his personal passion for gardening and could provide fresh vegetables for a few widows in the church. Better yet, he could set these widows up with a tomato or strawberry plant barrel that they could tend and enjoy with minimal effort. A senior who is (or was) a professional elementary school teacher might be a tutor for underprivileged, inner city children during the school year or over the summer. If by chance the last thing such a senior would be interested in doing as personal ministry is teaching children, she might serve others through her personal passion for artistic painting as a hobby by teaching and encouraging painting therapy at several senior living communities or at a local community center or branch library.

Regardless of what the service activities might be, the point is that exceptional seniors ministry helps encourage and provide age-specific opportunities for seniors to use their unique and personal giftedness in service to others. Whether that opportunity involves prayer, encouragement, gardening, artistic painting, or something else, they are examples of age and situation specific service opportunities around which personal ministry efforts can be built. They are service opportunities which others (seniors and non-seniors alike) can rally around in a joint effort and that are meaningful and authentically important services in God's kingdom.

CHAPTER NINE
An Oasis In The Desert
(*weekly devotionals at senior living communities*)

Confessions Of An Activities Director
Several years ago I was asked by a friend to contact an activities director who was trying to find churches interested in taking turns to provide weekly devotionals for her residents. As the activities director of this new facility, she was still developing the activities program. One thing that was missing was arranging for churches to provide weekly devotional visits. Some of the residents had requested this. It was also something she personally wanted to include.

When I met with her, she explained how she had been experiencing some difficulty finding any churches willing to provide weekly devotionals at the facility. At the end of our meeting, I told her I'd be happy to begin meeting with any of the interested residents on a weekly basis. Tears literally ran down her face as she confided how she had "*called 30 churches*" in the area. She had been turned down 30 times for various reasons (too busy with other commitments, don't have anyone readily available to send, simply not interested, etc.). Her tears were those of frustration as well as tears of joy and relief. Ironically, I was given a double opportunity that day – an opportunity to minister to a deeply wounded soul and an *opportunity* to become an oasis in the desert for some thirsty souls in a senior living community.

On another occasion, the activities director of a different senior living community called my home church with a similar request hoping to arrange for several churches in the area to visit their residents regularly on a rotating basis. When I offered to participate, they asked me to take the first month, which I did. When I asked (near the end of the month) who else had chosen to become involved, she regretfully confessed that no other churches had yet stepped up. I offered to take the next month or until she was able to arrange for other churches to participate. That was nearly five years ago and this community is still in need of additional participating churches.

Since I first began visiting these and other senior living communities weekly, the residents (as well as their activities directors, executive directors, nurses, and other staff members) have repeatedly and enthusiastically expressed their gratitude. Through the years senior residents, time and time again, have come up to me and made such statements as, *"I've missed going to church so much since I've moved here - until you began coming each week"* and *"You have no idea how much we appreciate the effort you make to visit us like you do."* Ironically, in the midst of even state-of-the-art facilities where seniors may be receiving top-notch *physical* health care, their *spiritual* needs are not being addressed. Providing spiritual nourishment and encouragement for such seniors in such situations is like providing them an oasis in the desert.

The Value Of Weekly Visits

The value of visiting senior living communities regularly is incalculable. For seniors who may otherwise be cut off from attending church, it is literally throwing them a spiritual lifeline of fellowship, encouragement, and spiritual nourishment. The need for regular, meaningful, personal fellowship, as well as group Bible study, doesn't "go away" simply because one moves from a residential home into community living with other seniors where they are, for all practical purposes, homebound. Quite the contrary, it's during the latter years that they most need regular, meaningful, personal fellowship, encouragement, and group Bible study for spiritual nourishment!

Seniors need spiritual encouragement most when they have experienced a significant loss (spouse, sibling, or peer). They need spiritual encouragement most during the incremental loss of their health. They need spiritual encouragement most during the loss of some or even much of their independence (and with that, their dignity ... piece by piece). They need spiritual encouragement most during the loss of such things as regular social contact, their private home residence, their ability to drive, and even the loss of their ability to attend their church home. It is neither the time nor the place for churches and church leaders to make minimal efforts, but rather is a time and a place to step up our efforts and devote more time, attention, and resources in outreach for such seniors in such circumstances.

Kinds Of Visits

Being a spiritual oasis in the desert for residents at senior living communities can be as simple as organizing a small group of a few church friends for singing hymns, reading scripture, and leading a prayer at each weekly visit. You may even take it upon yourself to "fly solo" as a "one man band." Believers should not underestimate just how much even one individual's faithful, weekly efforts are appreciated and enjoyed by seniors in such a facility. Depending on one's level of skills and confidence, an individual who faithfully tends to the ministry needs of such seniors could serve, essentially, in a "chaplain" capacity. Speaking from personal experience over several years, even the efforts of a single individual are warmly welcomed. If being a "one man band" is necessary in the beginning of your efforts, you are still an oasis in the desert for seniors who are thirsty for and in need of such loving, spiritual attention.

Ideally, however, being an oasis in the desert for residents at senior living communities would include a *group* effort, where at least a handful of believers (preferably consisting of all ages) make an even more effective *collective* effort. A *group* effort by several church members may also prove a more comfortable and enduring "fit" for numerous reasons. First, as an *officially recognized* part of the scheduled, weekly calendar of activities (rather than merely dropping in unexpectedly and unannounced, as an individual could do), you might be able to minister to some who would otherwise not be reached by an individual's efforts. Second, everyone (you, as well as attending residents) receives the benefits of a *group dynamics* effect that cannot be experienced when visiting individuals. Third, a group environment is more conducive to scripture based teaching and encouragement (in contrast to conversational chit-chat about the weather or ailments in a one-on-one visit). Fourth, it encourages friendships, fellowship, and spiritual camaraderie among residents that might not otherwise occur.

Fifth, as an officially recognized activity of the senior living community, it helps avoid accidentally visiting individuals at times that might conflict with other scheduled activities at the facility. Sixth, it likely substantially lengthens the quantity of the quality time spent with seniors. Whereas an individual chaplain style visit might last five minutes, a group devotional could last 20 to 45 minutes. Seventh, it creates an opportunity to minister (at least indirectly) to staff members who may be within "ear range" of the devotional. Group devotional visits and individual chaplain visits, however, are not mutually exclusive. It's not a matter of having to choose one or the other. In fact, they can reinforce each other. As relationships develop within a group devotional setting, opportunities for more personal, individual visits are natural outgrowths. For example, when a regular participant is unable to attend that week's group devotional, whether due to health reasons, discouragement, or even forgetfulness, this is an excellent time to make a personal visit.

Staff Approval and Support

Visiting individual residents in a senior living community whom you already personally know or who are members of your home congregation may only require "signing in" at the front desk as a visiting guest, but it usually doesn't involve requiring anyone's permission and authorization. However, before beginning any *group* ministry outreach effort, it's not only necessary, but it's also *useful* to obtain permission from the activities director as well as the executive director of the facility. Gaining the proactive support and involvement of the activities director, the executive director, and even other staff members for reminding residents on the scheduled day of the group visit and for helping gather the residents just prior to the time of your weekly visits only enhances your efforts.

At times I have called ahead much earlier in the day while at other times I've called while in route before the scheduled time to meet as a reminder for staff to help gather residents for the devotional. In some cases I've had an activities director gratefully say, *"Oh, is that today? Thanks for the heads-up!"* Other times, I've had them say, *"Oh, they're already gathered and anxiously waiting for you to arrive."* Experience has proven that once the routine has been established, most participating residents will simply show up eagerly (if you're actually offering substantial friendship and spiritual encouragement). However, especially in the beginning and even in an ongoing capacity, staff can play an extremely helpful role in reminding and encouraging participation among the residents. They can do this not only with regular attendees but also with new residents.

Milk or Meat

Another idea for a group effort, besides hymnal songs, scripture reading, and prayer, is to provide some occasional entertainment on special occasions by periodically utilizing the skills and giftedness of church friends. This might include those who can play the guitar or piano. It might include a "skit" or "drama" presented by the youth group or someone simply reading poetry. It could include an artist who paints such things as scenery, portraits, and caricatures or a craftsman who makes hand-made crafts. The sky is the limit when we begin using as much innovation and creativity for ministry with seniors as we have traditionally done with youth ministry.

Being a spiritual oasis for seniors can be as simple as singing, scripture reading, and prayer with occasional special activities or it can be even more. It can also include a short but "meaty" devotional lesson for encouragement and inspiration. Speaking from personal experience, a format that includes a "devotional lesson" is one that has been exceptionally well received. It has been one which has received unsolicited but very positive feedback from residents and numerous others, including activities directors, executive directors, receptionists, nurses, other attendants, relatives of residents, and any other individuals who have had an occasion to sit in, listen to, or simply overhear portions of the devotional.

Topics vs. Textual

Choices for devotional lessons could be topical (whether chosen by you or requested by senior residents) or textual. I personally prefer and would highly recommend a textual series (e.g. going through a book of the Bible) for several reasons. Topical studies can be quite valuable, highly informative, and very interesting, but they have two distinct potential disadvantages in this setting. First, trying to come up with a new topic week after week after week can become quite troublesome rather quickly, depending on the teacher's skill and experience level.

I've been involved in ministry for over 30 years and the thought of having to continually come up with "topics" week after week after week sounds exhausting – even for me! One exception to this is the use of study guide booklets for various topics. This might, however, require providing copies of the booklets for all the residents. To ensure full participation among the residents and to avoid unintentionally excluding those who could not afford to purchase one, you should offer these booklets to all residents at no cost, if they are needed or wanted by residents for the study.

A second possible disadvantage to using a topical study is that topics can more easily lend themselves to controversy, disharmony, and disunity than textual studies. This is especially true when ideas are submitted by residents. As helpful as topics might be, the primary objective should always be edification, encouragement, and inspiration. A textual series more easily ensures fulfilling this objective than does a topical study. This is not to say that controversial subjects should be avoided. It is to say that especially early in developing relationships of trust and credibility with the residents, it is wiser to focus more on common ground than controversy. Furthermore, any time controversial subjects are addressed (and they can come up even in a textual series), it's always far wiser to address them as gracefully as possible. You must remember that your primary objective is to edify and encourage, not turn off and turn away seniors. Weekly devotionals with seniors in a senior living community should never be used merely as an opportunity to have theological debates.

For these reasons I prefer textual series studies over topical ones. In order to maximize their usefulness, the studies you provide or personally develop for seniors should be as equally applicable for seniors living in an independent living community as they are for those living in assisted living facilities and those living in a full service health care center. However, the length of the meeting and the depth of the devotional time spent together may need to be adjusted for each. Residents in an assisted living facility may prefer and enjoy a brief but more "meaty" devotional lesson along with the singing and prayers, whereas seniors in a full health care facility, with greater physical limitations, may prefer and enjoy mostly singing.

Getting Initially Acquainted With The Residents
In the first meeting, it is a good idea to give everyone an opportunity to become a little better acquainted. It is as foolish to presume that residents know each other simply because they live in the same facility as it is to presume that everyone in a residential neighborhood knows their neighbors simply because they all lived on the same street. I prefer to use this first meeting as an "ice breaker" by introducing myself in a personable way (not just my name but where I'm originally from, my personal hobbies and interests, etc.) and then asking everyone else to do the same. This lays the cornerstone for building a foundation for friendship, fellowship, and

camaraderie for all (i.e. I can get to know them while they get to know me, and as they get to know each other). After everyone has shared a little about themselves, it is appropriate to offer a preview of what they can look forward to beginning with next week's visit (e.g. *"Next week, we'll begin a devotional study in the book of Mark."*).

Holy Hugs

An important part of weekly devotional visits includes giving to each attending resident a hug as well as a kiss on the cheek or forehead. By "important," I don't mean as perceived by *me* but as valued by the *residents*. Seniors have said such things as, *"I've been waiting all day for my hug"* and *"that's the first hug I've had all day."* From the moment I walk into the room where seniors are usually already gathered for the devotional, I immediately begin giving out holy hugs while making conversation with everyone there.

I have observed through the years that one of the things seniors enjoy most about the weekly devotional visits is ... the hug! In fact, some professionals have identified this extraordinary receptivity to human touch as "skin hunger." Residents enjoy the singing and appreciate the prayers as well as the devotional lessons. They always get a big kick out of any humor I share, but they *love* the holy hugs. Incidentally, I'm an "equal opportunity hugger." I hug the men, too (while also shaking their hand). Depending on how many seniors are present, hugs may take a few moments; but I take whatever time is necessary to personally greet each and every senior with a holy hug, not only as I arrive but also when I'm about to leave so that every senior attending receives two hugs per visit. In the many years that I've been visiting seniors at senior living facilities and the thousands of hugs I've given, I only recall two or perhaps three occasions when a senior declined a hug – which is an astounding percentage. Such statistics are very insightful and instructive about the need for and the value of the "holy hug." On those rare occasions, when a senior was a little too hesitant to accept a hug, at least the gesture of love was offered unconditionally and irrespective of acceptance ... just as God does for us all.

For a senior living community where you've just begun to visit, it might be advisable to wait a few weeks until after you've made several visits and had an opportunity to begin building a relationship with the residents before offering hugs. How soon you begin giving out holy hugs depends somewhat on your personality and the rapport established during the first few meetings. It also depends somewhat on your own personal comfort level with hugging others. Regardless of *when* to begin, hugging may take you a little outside your comfort zone unless you're already a "hugger". When you think the time has come, you might teasingly give them a "warning" that you will begin giving out holy hugs soon to those who give you permission. You might even take the opportunity to briefly discuss how an early church custom included greeting fellow believers with a *"holy kiss,"* as mentioned in scripture (Rom. 16:16). Regardless of when you actually begin your "holy hugging

132

ministry," ask each *individual* for approval in the presence of the entire group (i.e. not merely the group for *group* approval). As I ask each individual senior for permission, I step back slightly to use subtle "body language" for communicating a message that assures them that it's okay to decline a hug.

It is important to always ask for permission from *each individual* resident that first time for their first hug out of respect for anyone who may be uncomfortable with being hugged by a stranger. It would be discourteous, presumptuous, and overbearing, even in the name of God, to force such affection upon anyone who might not welcome it or could simply be a little too uncomfortable with it (at least until they've had some time to warm up to the idea by seeing all the other seniors receiving and enjoying their holy hugs). Long after you've established the custom and routine of regularly giving out hugs at a senior living community, it is also important to remember that whenever a "new" attendee comes to a devotional for the first time that you also obtain permission from that new attendee that first time (rather than simply begin hugging them too). However, once anyone has given permission that first time (which they almost always do), I humorously "warn" them that I won't ask again (i.e. at any future weekly devotional), but rather will simply presume from this point forward that I have their standing permission (which usually causes wide grins, sparkling eyes, and gleeful chuckles among all the residents).

If you're not naturally a "hugger," consider this a challenge to *grow* yourself as well as an opportunity to become a huge blessing to others in an undervalued way. *Resist* any reluctance you may have to giving out holy hugs. Resist any initial feelings to excuse yourself from learning to minister to seniors in this very grace-dispensing and much needed way. If, however, giving out hugs just isn't your "cup of tea," then by all means, feel free to forego giving out hugs. However, because of how much of a blessing hugs are to seniors, I would strongly encourage you to see this as an opportunity to take a bold step of faith outside your comfort zone for the sake of blessing others.

Transitional Small Talk

Immediately after the hugs and as I'm settling into a chair, I usually have less than a minute of transitional small talk. I prefer sitting in a chair rather than standing behind a podium even if a podium is available because a casual environment is more conducive for building relationships. This transition may only last a few seconds and usually consists of little more than a passing comment about the weather or a brief inquiry about how their week has been, what they've been up to, or if they been on any outings. I may also briefly share some interesting or trivial incident that may have occurred in my life during the past week (i.e. working in the flower beds, grandson made the varsity baseball team, etc.). This small talk serves as a transition from the hugging to the next activity. It also provides residents an opportunity to share something that may be on their minds or hearts (such as prayer requests or perhaps some trivial or even significant happenings in their lives or at the facility).

Brief Entertainment

Before beginning the actual "devotional" part of the visit, I take a few moments to provide some brief "entertainment." I personally prefer to use humor for several reasons. First, it's a relatively quick and easy resource. Second, it's usually a short form of entertainment that's simple to share. Third, seniors need and love humor in their lives. Finally, using humor week after week is a durable form of entertainment that requires a minimal amount of preparation because it demands no serious level of "talent" or assistance from others. However, even the simplest humor offers a breath of fresh air for residents who might need a good laugh or chuckle.

Any other form of brief entertainment, however, is equally excellent, such as a barber shop quartet singing a couple of songs, a musician playing the guitar, a pianist playing the piano, a magician performing a couple of tricks, a ventriloquist performing with his dummy, an impersonator doing his routine, poetry reading, or any other delightful form of entertainment. Most of the above mentioned alternatives can prove to be more difficult to use, especially on a *regular* basis. However, they would be superb for periodic, special occasions. For the "long haul," which is what weekly devotionals at senior living facilities are about (and what seniors at senior living communities need), short bits of humor are probably the simplest and most workable form of entertainment for bringing a little joy into the hearts and lives of seniors.

If your *primary* objective is to provide a weekly, inspirational devotional, the use of simple humor also helps the *devotional* remain the primary focus of your efforts. Coordinating more elaborate entertainment week after week can easily become a consuming distraction that overshadows your primary objective. It is likewise easier to delegate the task to fellow workers if all they are doing is sharing a little bit of humor rather than playing a musical instrument or performing an actual comic routine. You could even gather and give them the humorous material to simply read. For these reasons I prefer to simply use bits of humor for the entertainment portion of our visit on a week to week basis.

Kinds Of Humor

Seniors enjoy the silly humor almost as much as the holy hugs. The humor I share is nothing special, elaborate, or professional. It is simply material I've gathered through the years over the internet as friends have forwarded material to me. Just imagine ... all those silly emails that have been cluttering up your email box after giving you a brief chuckle can now actually serve an additional purpose! There are also some websites that offer free jokes and puns.

When gathering humorous resources, it is important to use audience and age appropriate humor. By audience appropriate, I simply mean take into consideration the mental ability of the residents. Many of the seniors I visit who live in assisted living communities can usually appreciate more complex humor such as a short story that must be carefully followed to get the punch line or where there may be a clever play on words. Other residents I visit live in full service health care facilities and may have more difficulty following such elaborate humor. The humor should also be age appropriate. By this I mean two things. First, use humor that references things with which seniors are familiar. For example, if the humor requires a familiarity with computer jargon and internet etiquette, it's probably not very age appropriate for seniors in a health care facility who may have never used a computer. By age appropriate I also mean not using humor that is degrading to age. Even when "no harm was intended," degrading humor is still degrading, whether it's an "old joke," a gender joke (the "dumb blonde") or some other stereotypical ethnic joke such as the "drunk Irishman," the "dumb Pollock" or the "penny pinching Jew."

Humor that is both audience and age appropriate may be a short story or a few "one-liners." It could be something new or something "as old as the hills and twice as dusty." Seniors enjoy them all. It doesn't have to be "professional" humor worthy of Seinfeld or Leno. In fact, it doesn't always have to be humor. I primarily use humor because laughter, as they say, is good medicine (Prov. 17:22), but occasionally I use such things as intriguing special stories or the etymological origin behind certain well known words and phrases. There are books that tell the story behind the writing of great hymns that are also fascinating to hear. Paul Harvey's "The Rest of the Story" material also provides wonderful alternatives. For many years I enjoyed reading a newspaper column by L.M. Boyd who shared unusual and little known trivia. A bookstore could provide even more resources for humor and other entertaining material.

She Finally Cracked A Smile Just As I Was About To Break A Sweat
I'll never forget the first time I began visiting the *healthcare side* of a senior living facility. Up until this time I had only been making weekly group devotional visits at *assisted living* communities where the residents are, as a general rule, in better physical health and are more mentally alert. After warmly greeting the residents and introducing myself, I launched into the brief humorous entertainment portion of my weekly visit. Much to my surprise, after delivering the first humorous line, there were no chuckles – not even one muffled snicker … nothing – not even as much as an obligatory half-smile. Taken somewhat off guard but having full confidence in the "material" (since I had used it with great success elsewhere), I pressed on with the next joke. Again, my attempt at humor "fell flat" and was met with stone silence, as well as with blank faces. The residents were mentally lucid and alert, although they were mostly wheelchair bound and especially physically frail.

At this point (and batting zero for two), my mind was racing ahead, even as I began to launch with a third attempt at humor. For the first time in my life, I *experientially* understood what it must feel like for a comedian facing a tough crowd to "bomb out" with his comedic routine. But I pressed on, knowing the value of humor, as well as my commitment to brighten their day if only in a small way. Even as I was launching my third attempt at some humor, I was hastily re-evaluating my "game plan" – determined to bring some light-heartedness to these seniors but prepared to accept defeat, lick my wounds, and proceed rather hastily straight into some hymn singing. As the words to my third attempt at humor were still lingering in the air, I noticed an ever so slight smile cracking out of the corner of the mouth of one side of one resident's otherwise totally somber face. At that point, I knew I "had them." It was all the encouragement I needed to press on.

In the weeks and months to come, those dear souls learned not only to smile but to chuckle and even laugh out loud. At times I came to hear them even repeat the "punch line" under their breath as they literally relished the humor. Something as simple and silly as sharing a little humor has brought some of these seniors back to "the land of the living" and given them a reason to smile again, if only for a little while. God taught me several significant lessons that day. I may have already had the "head" knowledge or have even known it instinctively, but He "brought it home" to me in a very real and experiential way. He reminded me of the value of humor. He reinforced the importance of perseverance, and perhaps most importantly, He vividly affirmed to me that even in a "state-of-the-art" healthcare facility, residents can become so withdrawn from life in hopelessness and despair that they can all but lose touch with such fundamental needs as joy, laughter, and a reason to smile.

Hymnal Singing

After the entertainment portion of the group visit, we sing songs from a hymnal. Some senior living communities may have hymn books on hand while at others this may not be the case. For facilities that do have hymnals, some residents will sing along, while others may only listen or faintly "lip sync" by memory. Even among those who do not sing, it is not uncommon to see some subtle toe tapping and hand patting to the faster songs. Whether or not seniors are singing along or simply "listening along," they are being blessed – and more importantly, God's priority for seniors is being honored.

For senior living communities that don't have any hymnals but where residents who are able wish to sing along, you can bring song books for everyone to use. An alternative is to make large print copies of some of the most well known favorites plus a few newer ones, assemble multiple sets, and keep each "notebook hymnal" in a simple binder/folder for each resident to use. Another option is to simply allow them to sing along as best they can by memory. They usually have little trouble singing along by memory with the more familiar favorites, especially when using the well known "first and last verses." Many hymns have a memorable chorus or often repeated "hook" to the song that most can sing along to by memory.

I try to use a mixture of old favorites and less familiar ones as well as slower and faster hymns. I also invite any requests from the seniors. Each kind of song has its value. The older ones are more familiar and probably most cherished as they bring back good memories from earlier days. Newer hymns or even more contemporary songs may be less known (or even completely new to them), but these offer a healthy mental and spiritual challenge for the residents as well as a freshness to the devotional experience that older hymns cannot do. The slower hymns can provide peaceful reminders of assurance, while faster ones can offer more spiritual stimulation.

Although I am no longer compelled to feel limited to the theological position of my religious heritage (which has a conviction about using *a capella* music exclusively), I mostly use *a capella* singing more out of convenience than conviction. If, however, there are any senior residents who are able to play hymns on the piano, I encourage them to play a song or two as part of the beginning of the devotional. Then, after singing several songs *a capella*, I personally choose to always use "Into My Heart" as a transitional song to the devotional lesson. Just prior to singing "Into My Heart," a simple transitional comment such as, *"And now our song before our prayer"* is appropriate. It's a simple song that everyone can do from memory without being "glued to" a songbook. This also allows me, while still singing, to be gathering my Bible and notes in preparation for a smoother, transition to the devotional lesson. At the end of the song, we have a short prayer.

Prayer
Just before the devotional lesson, we pray together. Occasionally seniors have made specific prayer needs known at this time. You might ask if there are any requests. Sometimes they have already made prayer requests known shortly after my arrival. I have always led the prayers myself or had a co-worker do so because most group devotionals usually consist primarily of women. The current generation of seniors is generally not accustomed to women leading "public" prayers, especially in the presence of men. I personally have no conviction against women participating in the leading of group prayers, but I have never invited it. I do so because most of these seniors would probably decline. I also want to avoid any unnecessary anxiety on the part of any seniors present who might have such scruples. If, however, one of the ladies offered or perhaps asked to lead a prayer, I would welcome it. The kind of prayers I prefer for a group devotional in this setting are relatively short and filled with praise and thanks.

Devotional Thought or Devotional Lesson
After a prayer, the remaining time together can consist of either a devotional thought or a complete lesson. If each weekly visit is built primarily around singing, a

devotional *thought* at or near the end of the singing can provide encouragement as well as a spiritual "nugget" of nourishment for seniors. Whoever is sharing the devotional thought for the week can easily transition into this part of the visit by simply saying something such as, "*We have one more song we'd like to sing, but before we do, we'd like to leave you with a devotional thought for the day.*" The devotional thought could be read, or perhaps if the one sharing the devotional thought feels capable, a few additional personal comments could be added. A devotional thought could be as brief as only a few seconds, if you're merely conveying an inspirational "one-liner" quote, or it could be a minute or two. Some good resources for devotional thoughts can be found in daily devotional books (such as Oswald Chambers' *My Utmost For His Highest*), daily devotional calendars, or even quotes from such notable characters as Mother Teresa or Billy Graham.

On the other hand, a complete devotional *lesson* could be as long as 10-20 minutes depending on the preference of the teacher. For lesson devotionals, it's important that whoever is giving the devotional lesson take their responsibility seriously by preparing as if they were teaching a class at the church building on a Sunday morning for any other age group. The last thing aging seniors in a senior living community deserve is to be offered an ill prepared, "go through the motions" devotional lesson where sufficient time in preparation wasn't given for making the lesson as encouraging, inspiring, applicable, and informative as possible. In addition to any concerns about the *quality* of the devotional is the *length*. Seniors, whose ability to sit for long periods of time may be limited, should not be expected to sit through too long a lesson. The objective is for them to be encouraged and refreshed by the devotional. They should be eager for next week, not exhausted from the experience of enduring it.

As discussed earlier in this chapter, devotional lessons can either be topical or textual. Historical narratives such as any of the "gospels" are good possibilities. The books of Acts, Genesis and Exodus are other excellent alternatives. I prefer what I call "a devotional approach," where the objective is not merely to convey information but to provide inspiration. I also make a deliberate attempt to use examples, draw analogies, and give illustrations that are specifically applicable and relatable to seniors. If, for example, a scripture text presents an opportunity to discuss the virtue of patience, I'd be less inclined to illustrate it by discussing the patience-testing challenge of traffic jams than I would to reference how exasperating it can be to wait on their facility's maintenance man to come and resolve some problem in their room.

A Hurry- Free, No-Rush Zone

Regardless of whether the devotional study is topical or a textual series, my suggestion is to t-a-k-e y-o-u-r t-i-m-e and not be in a rush when working your way through the study material. There's not necessarily any need to finish a topic in a six or nine week time-frame (simply because it's a six or nine week lesson booklet).

138

Similarly, a textual series doesn't have to be completed within a certain time frame either (i.e. an entire chapter each week). This is not to say that the devotional lessons should be needlessly lengthened with useless and irrelevant "fluff." Neither would you want to become bogged down with too much detail. It's simply to say that unless you're planning a *temporary* ministry effort with seniors, you're in this for the long haul. There is no need to rush through the study material by any self-imposed, arbitrary deadlines. In fact, the sooner you finish one topic or text, the sooner you'll just have to come up with another.

For example, if you planned to study the book of Mark with a group of seniors at a senior living community, you could either take a quicker *survey* of the text and be finished with the entire book of Mark in a few weeks – or you could take what I call a *textual devotional* approach and have several months worth of material. Surveys are an excellent method of Bible study and offer a valuable "bird's eye" perspective of scripture that only a survey can offer. However, by their very nature, they take less time and are not as devotional friendly because of their swifter, more fact-focused overview approach. What seniors in a senior living community need most is not some brisk, academic summary of scripture as much as a more thoughtful, devotional approach.

When I use the term "textual devotional approach", I do not mean a more tedious "verse by verse" study. Rather, it's just an unrushed and more reflective, *section-by section* approach with no particular time frame in mind. A quicker outline understanding of some book in the Bible is marvelous for theologians, scholars, and college students, but it isn't as likely to encourage and inspire aging seniors as would a slower devotional look at scripture. Perhaps for a younger generation that is often over-stimulated, impatient, and short on time, sermons and Bible classes might need to move at a more rapid pace in order to "connect" with the audience and retain their attention. However, a group devotional at a senior living community is a time when seniors no longer have to rush, nor care to rush. It's also a place where devotional leaders have a golden opportunity to slow down and "decompress" as they lead the devotional. A textual devotional approach with seniors meets the ministry needs of seniors more effectively. It may also prove to be a "therapeutic" opportunity for a usually frazzled devotional leader to experience a weekly refreshing reprieve from a fast-paced world.

Thinking Beyond "Senior Issues"

If a topical approach is used, another important consideration (and personal recommendation of mine) is to think *beyond* merely using "senior issues." Loneliness, discouragement, depression, failing health, and so forth are some of the more predictable issues some might consider especially applicable for seniors. However, they are not the only possibilities and are probably not the best place to begin. Ironically, in an effort to use what some might think is more "relevant"

139

material, concentrating on such "senior topics" is not, in my opinion, what seniors need most from a weekly devotional, even though this may seem contrary to conventional wisdom. Unless an individual senior is critically, clinically depressed, I believe a more proactive, preventive approach is a better way to address such senior issues than a more reactive, "curative" one. If a senior is clinically depressed, he needs a professional more than a devotional level of attention than can be provided in a group devotional setting anyway. However, if he's not clinically depressed, he will more likely be better served by using more of a "preventive" than "curative" tactic.

An Ounce of Prevention Is Worth A Pound of Cure
We understand this principle *outside* the context of seniors and seniors ministry. It's usually considered common sense that one of the best ways to minister to someone with a non-clinical personal issue, regardless of age, is to help them stop thinking about *themselves* and begin thinking *outside* of themselves. Such an outward focus can help resolve their problems more effectively than any amount of "lessons" could ever hope to do. For example, we could try to teach "lessons" about loneliness and discouragement to lonely and discouraged teens or young adults but we would likely see few positive results. However, a much better idea is to address their "pity party" by redirecting their attention toward helping others. The sooner they begin to focus on others instead of themselves, the sooner they can begin feeling and *being* better. "Lessons" on loneliness and discouragement taught "at" them become unnecessary and may even compound the problem. A steady diet of lessons on "*how to fix me and my personal issues*" will not likely be helpful. Directly teaching and talking about personal "issues" certainly have their place but that's only one way and not necessarily the best way to help.

Which would likely be the more uplifting approach for encouraging and inspiring struggling, single parent moms? Would merely, primarily, and only talking *at* them about the issues and challenges of being a single parent in a "lesson" kind of way be the most effective? Would not reminding them about the faithfulness of God while challenging and inspiring them to live a life of faith in God and service to others, even in the midst of their struggles, be more effective? Which would likely be the more helpful and effective approach to encourage and inspire broken-home and broken-hearted divorcees? Would merely, primarily, and only talking *at* them about the issues and challenges of being divorced in a "lesson" kind of way? Would not reminding them about the goodness of God while challenging and inspiring them to walk by faith and reach out in service to others, even in the midst of their struggles, be more beneficial? Certainly, there is a time and a place for single parent moms to discuss and perhaps even "study" about their unique issues, challenges, and needs, as there is for divorcees to do the same. However, the more effective way to spiritually bless struggling single-parent moms, wounded divorcees or depressed, lonely, and discouraged seniors is to help them begin thinking *beyond* their own personal issues.

A Well Rounded Spiritual Diet Is The Best "Cure"

Paul told Timothy that *"ALL scripture"* (not just verses applicable to our personal issues, challenges, and problems) is profitable for making us complete (2 Tim. 3:16). It may be helpful to occasionally focus on "senior issues" with seniors, but what they need most is to be treated just like any other believer with personal issues and challenges. What they need most is the encouragement and inspiration that can come from a well-rounded "diet" of Bible study. Just like single moms need spiritual nourishment and nurturing for more than merely personal, single-parent issues and challenges of life – and just like divorcees need spiritual nourishment and nurturing for more than merely personal, broken-home issues and challenges of life – seniors likewise need spiritual nourishment and nurturing for more than merely "senior issues" or any age-related challenges that they may face during their senior years. In fact, it is by and through the very spiritual nourishing and nurturing they receive in all the other areas of their life that their personal, age related issues and challenges can most likely be seen in a broader context and become less of an issue.

Closing Prayer And Parting Hugs

After the devotional lesson is finished, my preferred way for wrapping up the visit is with another brief prayer along with some parting goodbye hugs for every senior at the devotional. This way, every senior receives two hugs during each visit – at the beginning as well as at the end. It is difficult to overemphasize just how meaningful and important the physical contact of a holy hug can be for seniors whose only "human contact" may otherwise be the medical care they receive from a nurse or a doctor.

Using these components for a weekly group devotional visit is certainly not the only way to provide exceptional ministry with seniors in a senior living community, but it is a format that has been well received and highly commended by residents and staff alike. This format is not just "a good idea in theory," but has been proven very effective for years. If replicating this format is helpful, then use it. Why reinvent the wheel? If, however, you find that another way works better for you, by all means use it. The main thing is that we not allow these seniors to be "left behind." We honor God's high priority for seniors by ministering to them, whether those seniors reside within our own congregation, our own neighborhood and city, or among the all but forgotten residents of senior living communities.

CHAPTER TEN

How Do You Spell Relief?

(caring for caregivers)

As has been repeatedly stated elsewhere in this book, ministry with today's seniors is not just about seniors. It's also very much about the adult *caregiving* children of aging seniors. Even if a congregation were to consist of absolutely no seniors (which isn't likely since, statistically speaking, half of all Protestant members are over 60), there would still be a need for seniors ministry – if only to provide support and encouragement for adult children of aging parents who may be struggling with their caregiving responsibilities.

A Growing Need

Caregiving has become an increasingly important aspect of American culture. Thanks to modern science, new medications, and advanced medical procedures, people are living longer. In times past, when the average lifespan was much less than today, the need to care for aging parents was not nearly the prominent issue that it has become now. With a growing number of individuals living well into their 80s and beyond, more and more adult children of seniors are faced with not only raising their own children but also with caring for their aging parents. In today's world, two married adults can easily find themselves needing to care for as many as four aging parents (in addition to any of their own children who may still be living at home). Those facing such a situation are sometimes called the "sandwich generation." In fact, because of the increased longevity factor, a few adult children of parents even find themselves in need of caring for their aging parents *and their grandparents* (referred to wittily by some as the "Dagwood Sandwich" generation).

Resources For Caregivers

Because caregiving has become such a prominent issue, there are already a growing number of resources available for adult children of aging parents which address caregivers' needs and issues. An exceptional seniors ministry program will certainly include compiling and providing helpful caregiving resources, whether in the form of books, CD's, or even occasionally arranging for guest speakers to address this area of need during special meetings or perhaps before the entire congregation.

Our objective is not to "reinvent the wheel" or reiterate information that's already readily available. Our objective is to focus on how caregiving fits in to the "big picture" of seniors ministry in the 21st century and more specifically into the seniors ministry opportunities and efforts of a church. We are assuming that those interested in providing exceptional ministry with seniors within their congregation can access these readily available resources by simply dropping by their local bookstore, consulting the American Association of Retired Persons (AARP), or surfing the internet. Rather, our objective here is to affirm that ministering to caregivers is an essential part of an exceptional seniors ministry program.

Connecting Caregivers with Caregivers

Caregiving can be a very consuming and overwhelming experience without a support system. Consequently, a good place for an exceptional seniors ministry program to begin to help caregivers is to first ensure that caregivers are connected with each other. It should not be presumed that all the caregivers in a congregation know about each other or necessarily seek each other out for mutual encouragement and moral support. Therefore, an intentional effort should be made to help all interested caregivers connect with each other. In fact, the single most important first step an exceptional seniors ministry program can do for caregiving adult children of aging seniors is to help them develop a caregiver's support group.

Just as self-help support groups are beneficial, perhaps even *essential* for those with family members struggling to cope with such addictions as alcohol and other drugs, a caregiver's support group can be similarly beneficial for adult children of aging parents. Such children often struggle to meet the exhausting physical and emotional demands that come with providing adequate and loving care for aging parents. Such participants can provide mutual encouragement for each other. They can also share helpful ideas and suggestions based upon personal experience. Caregivers need an opportunity where they can regularly share their struggles with others who not only care but *experientially* understand.

Forming or Finding A Support Group

Where there are numerous caregivers within a congregation, they can form a support group as a means of mutual encouragement and validation. However, with a limited number, they may need to find and become a part of some caregivers support group outside their home church by checking with other local congregations, community organizations, or local hospitals. Regardless of how it is done, a seniors ministry program that includes helping form or find a support group network for caregivers can spell the difference between deep despair and distress and the ability to "stay the course."

143

Connecting Caregivers With Non-Caregivers

After caregivers become more personally acquainted with each other, an exceptional seniors ministry program should identify ways in which *non*-caregiving volunteers can be involved with and more supportive of caregivers. Just as seniors ministry is about more than seniors, ministry with caregivers is about more than caregivers. If the ministry needs of caregivers are to be adequately addressed, a caregivers' ministry effort should also include encouragement from non-caregiving members. That assistance might come in the form of non-caregivers periodically sitting with the aging parents of caregivers for an afternoon or evening. The encouragement might come in the form of periodically accompanying caregivers to visit their parents in a care facility if only to provide moral support and to demonstrate how much you care. The supportiveness might come in the form of simply treating a caregiver to lunch or a movie from time to time as a healthy distraction. Obtaining non-caregiver volunteers requires what any other exceptional ministry program that is in need of volunteers requires – the enthusiastic backing of the church leadership. Publicly promoting seniors ministry efforts before the congregation is as essential to the success of an exceptional seniors ministry program as it is for any other ministry effort that churches and church leaders take seriously.

An announcement buried somewhere in the back of a weekly church bulletin will not suffice. Neither will a bland, one-time announcement sandwiched in the midst of a multitude of other announcements on a Sunday morning just as everyone is about to be dismissed. Rather, the effort to solicit volunteers for ministering to caregivers (or for any other aspect of an exceptional seniors ministry program) should be as earnest, appealing, and creative as it is when recruiting volunteers for the children or teen ministries. The need should be given the church's undivided attention whether "from the pulpit," in a special announcement, through personal testimonials, or even by means of a dramatization (such as I've seen done when a church was recruiting for youth and children ministry programs). An exceptional seniors ministry program will always aim for exemplary results, but such results usually require an extraordinary effort. If we intend to provide this kind of seniors ministry program, we must always go about it in an exceptional manner.

The more connected caregivers are with each other, the more likely it is that they will have their ministry needs met while concurrently helping meet the needs of their fellow caregivers. Likewise, the more aware and informed the non-caregiving members of the congregation are about the ministry needs of caregivers, the more help becomes available for meeting the ministry needs of exhausted and struggling caregivers. Caregivers can certainly connect with each other without the help of an exceptional seniors ministry program. In *theory*, their ministry needs can be met by fellow caregivers as well as by non-caregivers without an "official" ministry effort being provided by the church … just like the ministry needs of teens and children can be met without an "official" ministry effort being provided by the church. In *reality*, however, if we are serious about meeting the ministry needs of caregivers, we need to provide an exceptional seniors ministry program that intentionally reaches out to caregivers within the congregation and throughout the community.

CHAPTER ELEVEN
The Little Red Engine
(overcoming obstacles to moving forward)

Even with a clear understanding of the need for as well as the value, importance, and urgency of seniors ministry, proponents of *exceptional* seniors ministry will likely face some serious obstacles. Even with a clearly defined mission statement and a solid list of core values, those who are simply trying to encourage a more exceptional seniors ministry effort will almost certainly face certain barriers and resistance. When facing such inevitable obstacles and opposition, it's helpful to have given some *forethought* to the challenges that typically arise.

Understand, however, that there is no guaranteed resolution to any of the obstacles that may be encountered while encouraging churches and church leaders to start treating seniors ministry more like a priority than an afterthought. Furthermore, the odds are greater that the resistance will come in the more subtle and diplomatic form of good-sounding "reasons." Such reasoning might be expressed in such statements as *"We're limited in funds," "We feel we need to focus on other, more pressing/important needs," "The timing isn't right,"* or *"We think we're already making a sufficient effort."* They might also include such replies as *"We'll get back to you," "We'll form a committee to consider the matter further,"* and a seemingly endless array of other diplomatic maneuverings.

The more subtle and diplomatic the resistance, the more difficult it is to address that resistance without sounding, looking, and *feeling* like some extremist riding his "hobby horse." However, that is the whole tactical point of subtle, diplomatic resistance. Fortunately, the more forethought you've given to the most common forms of resistance the more effectively you can address it in a reasonable way. The more forethought you've given to obstacles and opposition, the more likely you may be able to open eyes, minds, and hearts for making them receptive to God's priority for seniors ministry. However, remember as you persevere that just as *"a mind is a terrible thing to waste,"* closed minds are a terribly difficult thing to open.

Budget Limitations
Although genuine budget limitations do exist, how often has that ever stopped a church from doing something they were *really* committed to doing? On both a personal and church level, a lack of funds is rarely the *real* issue at hand.

146

Occasionally it is, but it's the rare exception rather than the general rule. When it comes to limited church budgets and exceptional seniors ministry, it's usually not an issue of limited funding but *limited commitment*. It's usually not an issue of limited resources but *misplaced priorities*. We *find* a way to do the things that are *truly* important to us. As long as we're wandering in the wilderness of apathy, funding will always either inhibit or prohibit moving forward, whether we're talking about launching some new and exciting ministry outreach, building a new educational wing to the facilities, or developing an exceptional seniors ministry program. Once we resolve to faithfully embrace God's high priority for seniors as our own - once we resolve to move courageously beyond the apathy - once we resolve that it's no longer a matter of *if* but only a matter of *how*, funding issues have a way of simply resolving themselves.

Lest I appear too flippant or "Pollyannaish" about financial limitations, consider what a church that *"doesn't have the money in the budget"* would do if, during the middle of a blazing hot summer or the dead of winter, the church building's cooling or heating system suddenly and unexpectedly "gave up the ghost" and went to that great HVAC home in the sky. I can assure you that there would be a brand new A/C or furnace cooling or heating the building before the following Sunday – not because that church *"had the money in the budget for it,"* but because it would genuinely be a high priority of both the church leaders and the members. What *wouldn't* happen is that they would simply hope that "perhaps someday" they'd get it replaced. They wouldn't simply pay "lip service" to how important it is but then make it a "back burner" issue. They wouldn't form a committee to study it to death. They wouldn't be saying *"we think it's cool/warm enough in here already without it."*

Even when *"it's not in the budget,"* churches can and routinely do find numerous ways to do what's *important* to them. A wealthier member or two might step forward and simply pay the bill for replacing the worn out unit. Perhaps the church might take up a special contribution. I know of a family whose house unexpectedly burned down. They lost everything, but a few members (i.e. not even the entire church) took it upon themselves to help provide some relief for this hurting family. They did so by organizing a benefit concert with the help of some friends who were professional musicians. In a matter of days, they raised about $10,000 to help this hurting family begin piecing their life back together after that devastating fire. As the old saying goes, *"Where there's a will, there's a way"* ... but it starts with the *will*. If we have no godly passion for honoring this high priority of God's, the least we can do is be honest because it usually isn't a matter of money, but of priorities.

Other Competing, Pressing Needs

When seniors ministry is not seen as a *high* priority, experience has proven over and over again that there will always be an endless list of other competing, legitimate, and worthy causes that will continually arise and be seen as either more important or more urgent than seniors ministry. This is why so much time was spent discussing the need for as well as the value, importance, and urgency of seniors ministry in chapter one. Anytime something is seen as less important, in comparison to other needs, there's *never* a good time to begin giving it priority attention. As long as seniors ministry is viewed as *relatively* unimportant, other needs will always come before it because there is never enough time and money to do everything churches would like to do. Given such limitations, we are continually faced with making difficult choices about what and how much we can do and what must be left on the "back burner."

This is why the "battle" for exceptional ministry with seniors must center on the importance of seniors ministry. If we are not convicted in the heart and by the Spirit about God's high priority for seniors and seniors ministry, the prospects of taking seniors ministry more seriously are not good. The deceptive thing about other competing needs is that it doesn't have to be an "either/or" proposition. It's not God who makes us choose between paving more parking space and developing an exceptional seniors ministry program. We create that dilemma when we exchange God's priorities for our own. All that's really needed to begin with is a genuine, heart-felt, spirit-convicted commitment from church leaders to developing an exceptional seniors ministry program. However, it has to be an authentic commitment, not merely "*be ye warmed and filled*" lip service (Jm. 2:16). We have to courageously and faithfully journey out of the land of apathy for seniors ministry and into the land of *when* and *how* to begin treating God's high priority for seniors more like a priority than an afterthought.

Once a church and its leaders are truly convicted in the heart by the Spirit about making seniors ministry a high priority, it will happen. Funding will no longer be an obstacle. Trust me … better yet, trust God! Neither will interference from other pressing needs. Once a genuine commitment has been made and it's no longer a matter of "if" but only a matter of "when" and "how," the funds can be raised. They can be raised through some budget restructuring, a special contribution, or some creative fund raising event. Once church leaders are resolved to develop an exceptional seniors ministry program, interference from other pressing needs becomes irrelevant or at least too insignificant to matter.

Persistent interference may eventually require some rather adamant but cordial "*why not*" conversations" along with some firm but polite "*if not now, when*" discussions to "flush out" the obstacles and establish that commitment. As long as leaders are allowed to fall back on excuses, regardless of how legitimate they may sound or even be, the ministry needs of seniors will continue to go overlooked and underserved. Basically, any reply other than an unqualified "yes" will probably require suggesting a deadline, volunteering your input in the process, and informing them that you'll be following up with them by a certain date (to build in some "accountability"). Interference from other pressing needs is simply not a legitimate reason for allowing those other pressing needs to perpetually take precedence over the ministry needs of seniors.

"We're Already Doing Enough For Seniors"
In the highly unlikely event that this is actually true, such churches and church leaders are to be commended. Although some churches may be leading the way in making sufficient efforts in seniors ministry, far too many are not doing nearly enough. If, after reading the message of this book, you're inclined to think your home church is not doing enough, the odds are in your favor that you're probably right. When we think we're *"already doing enough"* with seniors, we most likely have a very limited perception of their needs. There is a fundamental need for churches, church leaders, and other believers to broaden their understanding and expand their definition of the ministry needs of seniors.

If *"already doing enough"* means that a church is already providing Bible classes and church services for seniors, then I am compelled to ask why this isn't also considered "sufficient" for youth ministry. If *"already doing enough"* means that seniors may already be receiving visits when in the hospital, then I am compelled to ask why this isn't also considered "sufficient" for youth ministry. If *"already doing enough"* means that church members are already surrounding seniors with love during the loss of a loved one, then I am compelled to ask why this isn't also considered "sufficient" for youth ministry? If *"already doing enough"* means that the church may already schedule occasional "potluck" dinners for them, then I am compelled to ask why this isn't also considered "sufficient" for youth ministry? If *"already doing enough"* means that the church may send seasonal fruit baskets during the holidays, then I am compelled to ask why this isn't also considered "sufficient" for youth ministry?

The point is not to pick on youth ministry but to see seniors ministry in the same light as we see other ministries that we treat as a high priority. The *real* problem is how little we value seniors as well as a basic lack of understanding about the ministry needs of seniors. We've broadened our understanding of the ministry needs of our youth since the middle of the last century. We need to broaden our understanding of the ministry needs of seniors, too. Meals, trips, and gifts merely scratch the surface for meeting the needs of our youth. No church or church leader in his right mind would call such minimal efforts "already doing enough." Meals, trips, and gifts likewise only scratch the surface for meeting the needs of seniors.

"We'll Get Back With You"
It may be that when you approach churches and church leaders about developing an exceptional seniors ministry program that they really will get back with you. You must, however, allow for the possibility that they won't – either because their good

intentions will be sidetracked by other important matters or perhaps because they hope to ignore you into oblivion. It reminds me of the infamous *"we'll see"* response of parents when a child asks about something the parents really hope will just go away if they ignore it long enough. Since nobody can read the hearts and motives of others, church leaders should be given the benefit of the doubt. Initially, they should be taken at their word and trusted that they will get back with you if they say they will.

However, a lesson from the fortieth president of the United States (Ronald Reagan) might prove both instructive and helpful at this point. During the "Cold War" with the Soviet Union, Reagan's personal approach to mutual disarmament of nuclear weapons of mass destruction with the former Soviet Union was *"trust, but verify."* Whenever a church or church leaders say they'll get back with you, trust that they will ... but verify it with tentative deadlines of accountability. Simply ask them approximately when you should expect to hear back from them. If you hear from them within this timeframe, great – but if not, then give them a call or send them an email for an update. Trust ... but verify.

Forming A Committee

A committee can be a good thing ... or not such a good thing. A committee can be a wonderful way to carefully research and discuss the need for an exceptional seniors ministry program. However, it can also be a convenient way to sidestep commitment by talking things to death and ultimately hi-jacking God's high priority for exceptional seniors ministry. If a church or church leaders intend to form a committee, you should ask to head it up or at the very least serve on it. In the spirit of *"nobody takes care of your business like you take care of your business,"* it's likely that the committee would benefit immensely from the presence and input of someone who is already seriously committed to seniors ministry. It's far more likely that seniors ministry will be given more serious consideration if someone is on the committee who has already read the message of this book and is both fully informed and highly motivated about the importance of providing exceptional ministry with today's seniors. Whether or not you are on the committee, provide the message of this book as a resource for every committee member.

Any Other Obstacles

It isn't practical to attempt to list every possible obstacle that might arise when trying to champion and promote exceptional seniors ministry. Fortunately, it isn't necessary. Regardless of what form the obstacle or opposition may take (postponements, delay tactics, political maneuvering, etc.), the resolution always comes back to two key things – priority and perseverance. If ministry with seniors is ever to be viewed and treated as more than an afterthought, it will be because someone begins pointing out the need for as well as the value, importance, and urgency of seniors ministry. In addition to clearly and convincingly establishing the priority of seniors ministry, keep persevering through all the obstacles and opposition.

CHAPTER TWELVE

Blah ... Blah ... Blah ...

(talk is cheap, so where do we go from here?)

Someone once said, "*After all is said and done, more is usually said than done.*"
Paul said essentially the same thing when he spoke of those who were "*ever learning
and never coming to a (useful) knowledge of the truth*" (2 Tim. 3:7). Just as Pilate
stood at a crossroads judging the fate of Jesus and asking "*What shall I do with
Jesus?*" (Mt. 27:12), everyone who reads the message of this book stands at a similar
crossroads and must make a decision. After coming to a more meaningful realization
of the importance of exceptional seniors ministry, it must be similarly decided what to
do with seniors and seniors ministry. What will you *do* with the message of this
book? Will you allow inaction to wishfully "*wash your hands of the matter*" as Pilate
had hoped to do - and in doing so essentially pronounce a "death sentence" on the
future of exceptional seniors ministry in your home church? Or will you boldly,
courageously, and faithfully take a step of faith forward for God's high priority for
seniors?

Ooops! A Re-Run

The story is told of the old visiting preacher who, after sharing an especially
important message on a Sunday morning from the pulpit and with neither warning nor
explanation, began preaching the exact same sermon that Sunday night. He used the
same introductory comments, the same scriptures, the same three major points, the
same illustrations, and the same conclusion. The further he went with his "re-run"
sermon, the more uncomfortable members became – not for themselves but for the
visiting preacher. You could almost feel the tension in the air as members began
squirming in their seats, glancing toward each other, embarrassed for the poor
forgetful soul, who they were collectively concluding must have experienced some
massive memory loss sometime between the morning and evening service.

Afterwards, members were hesitant to approach the kindly old preacher
concerning his embarrassing blunder, especially since he seemed completely
oblivious to it. Finally, one brave soul gingerly approached the preacher in the back
of the foyer and said, "*Preacher, don't you remember that you already did that*

sermon this morning?" ... to which the preacher quipped, *"Oh we all heard it this morning, but it's still yet to be done."* Hearing and knowing is one thing, but doing ... well, that's quite another. Even though the message of this book has been written ... and is being read, it's still yet to be *done*. Until we begin *doing* something about it, it's all just a bunch of words ... nice sounding words ... but just words - until we begin *doing* something about it.

Making A Transition From Hearing To Doing
Now that we've *heard* the message of this book, where do we go from here? Now that we've *heard* about the need for as well as the value, importance, and urgency of seniors ministry, where do we go from here? More importantly, what can *you* do to "get the ball rolling" in your own congregation? What's the next step in the adventure of establishing an exceptional seniors ministry within your home church ... and then beyond?

Share The Message
In addition to personally engaging in exceptional seniors ministry yourself, perhaps the first and foremost thing that can be done to promote exceptional ministry with seniors is to simply share the message of this book with others. Begin with other members of your home congregation who you think might possibly be open to re-thinking seniors ministry. Begin there ... but don't stop there. *Every* member of the congregation needs to become more aware of God's high priority for seniors, so share the message of this book even with those about whose level of interest in seniors ministry you may not even have a clue ... because this is more about God's high priority for seniors than it is about any individual's presumed interests or personal preferences. Furthermore, God's high priority for seniors needs to be embraced by the entire church, not just one or a few isolated individuals. It may need to be *led* by a "core group," but it needs to be embraced congregationally.

Loan them your copy of this book, or give them each their own copy. Express your desire for their thoughts and impressions afterwards (but suggest a time frame of, say, within the next week or two for their feedback). When deciding with whom to share this book, deliberately include members of *all* ages, from older seniors to younger seniors to middle-age adults to younger adults. Regardless of whether you think you may know how or what your church leaders may think about seniors ministry, include some if not *all* of them on the list of people with whom you share the message of this book. Church leaders especially need to hear the message because they will largely and ultimately affect how interested, involved, and supportive the entire congregation will be about providing exceptional seniors ministry.

It's especially important to proactively seek *feedback* from your church leaders rather than simply share the message of this book with them. If they agree with the message of this book, you need to know so that you can continue encouraging them to *do* something about it. If, however, after sharing the message of this book with them they don't readily see the importance of seniors ministry, you should try to discover why so you can help them begin navigating through the obstacles and the excuses. This way, together, you can begin moving forward. I say "moving forward" because once seniors ministry is seen as a high priority of God's, He will provide a way for you to help your home church move forward. He will clear a way for you to begin pursuing and honoring His priorities, regardless of the obstacles, reasons, and excuses you may face.

For God, there is no acceptable excuse for making His high priority for seniors a low priority. For God, there are no insurmountable obstacles to His priorities. For God, it's never a matter of *if* but only a matter of *how* and *when*. Never lose sight of the fact that churches and church leaders rarely find obstacles insurmountable when they consider something a high priority. For establishing an exceptional seniors ministry, "obstacles" are not the problem anyway. The *real* problem is actually the lack of priority. Once the "priority problem" is resolved, all the other "obstacles" will resolve themselves. Beyond your own individual efforts with seniors, your number one goal should be to help churches and church leaders see the high priority God has placed on seniors ministry.

Extend An Invitation

Another possible course of action can be to invite Sage Ministries to come and meet with your church and church leadership. This could occur either before or after your own individual efforts. Consulting others can offer a fresh perspective, as well as moral support for your efforts. In fact, the combined efforts of "insiders" and "outsiders" can provide a decisive "best of both worlds" advantage when trying to encourage churches and church leaders to begin placing a high priority focus on seniors ministry.

When *local* members encourage exceptional seniors ministry, they have the advantage of being already known and respected by the church and church leadership. However, they also have the disadvantage of being "*a prophet without honor in his own country*" - a formidable obstacle even Jesus Himself faced (Mt. 13:57). The same words and the same message coming from an outside source can sometimes make an impact that your very same words may not make on the church or the church leaders. However, just like an outside specialist may gain the attention and respect of a church and church leadership that a local member may not, even a savvy, outside consultant will always have a disadvantage, too. He is an "outsider" whom the church and church leaders don't personally know well enough to necessarily trust enough to act upon the information that is shared. An outside consultant will still be an outsider, regardless of how compelling the message. The combined efforts of both insiders and outsiders, however, could prove to be far more effective than the effort of either one without the other.

Remember, if the importance of exceptional seniors ministry was easy for churches and church leaders to grasp, such ministry programs would already be a high priority for churches and church leaders all over our nation. If it were that easy, we would have long ago seen a proliferation of exceptional seniors ministry programs popping up among churches, not so unlike what we've seen happen with youth ministry and other "favored" programs for the past 40 years. Helping your church and church leaders see the importance of seniors ministry can be a daunting and arduous task. You may need all the help you can get – so seek and welcome it.

In the business world, corporations seek outside resources and consultants all the time in the form of conferences, seminars, and other special corporate efforts. Churches and church leaders are also well accustomed to relying upon outside consultants. We routinely use an architect to help plan a new wing to the building, a fund raising specialist to pay for that expansion, thematic lectureships and workshops to educate and inspire believers, and church growth experts to help grow congregations. We're just not accustomed to doing so for things we have (subconsciously?) relegated to low priorities. Just because you begin sharing the message of this book, don't assume churches and church leaders will be readily open to using an outside consultant. If, however, it's important enough to rely upon outside specialists for building buildings and growing churches as well as teaching and inspiring members about other important matters through lectureships and workshops, why isn't it just as important to use outside specialists when it comes to God's high priority for seniors?

Schedule A Workshop

Another possible course of action can be to utilize our half-day workshop entitled "In Pursuit of God's Passion." The workshop and the promotional efforts leading up to it help establish and reinforce a high priority status for exceptional seniors ministry before the entire congregation and for those who attend the workshop. It is an excellent way to help a church see the importance of exceptional seniors ministry and begin treating seniors ministry more like a priority than an afterthought.

Regardless of whether one of the suggestions provided is your next step, what's important ... no, what's *critical* is that you take that next step – and the next one and the next one after that. To adapt a famous phrase, "*All it takes for the ministry needs of seniors to continue being overlooked and under-addressed is for good people to do nothing.*" All it takes for ministry with seniors to continue being treated more like an afterthought than a priority is ... nothing. Make a difference! Be the difference! Take that next step knowing that just by reading the message of this book and then sharing it with others, you've made a significant step toward helping your church and church leaders start honoring one of God's highest but more neglected priorities.

Teamwork and Cooperation

All it takes to begin making a difference is for one individual to take that next step, whether that next step involves personally involving yourself in ministry efforts with seniors, sharing this book with others, inviting us to come meet with your church and church leaders, or utilizing our half-day workshop. One individual can begin making a difference, but the more individuals you can encourage to become involved, the bigger difference you will collectively make. Making a *bigger* difference involves teamwork and cooperation. Whether in the business world, our personal life, or in our church ministry efforts, a healthy spirit of cooperation with others is essential for maximizing results – as a T E A M (Together Each Accomplishing More). It's axiomatic that "*the whole is always greater than the sum of its parts.*" Even scripture validates this principle (Eccl. 4:12). We recognize that exceptional ministry with other age groups requires it. Ministry with seniors requires no less. What does teamwork and cooperation look like for developing *exceptional* ministry with today's seniors?

It takes older seniors – Although less active seniors may feel like (or be viewed as) "recipients" more than as "contributors," even older seniors can still have a profound impact for the cause of Christ by simply finding less active but equally significant ways to remain meaningfully involved. Whether in the ministry of intercessory prayer or through the ministry of encouragement to others as previously discussed in Chapter 8, prayer can be a powerful ministry (Jm. 5:16), as can encouragement.

It takes younger seniors – Exceptional seniors ministry is not just about "older" seniors. Younger seniors have not only an opportunity to honor one of God's highest priorities (Ex. 20; Jm.1), but they also have a sacred responsibility to instill the same into the hearts and minds of succeeding generations (Tit. 2:4; 2 Tim. 2:2). If simply honoring God's priorities weren't sufficient incentive, "younger" seniors will eventually find themselves "older" seniors, too, and in need of being honored. If today's younger seniors, who will soon become tomorrow's older seniors, expect to be treated with "honor" when older, they must begin setting the precedence now by providing an inspiring example for younger generations to follow.

It takes teens and children – As has been stated repeatedly, seniors ministry is not just about seniors. Exceptional ministry with today's seniors is an intergenerational effort where all ages are involved and engaged in the lives and hearts of seniors. Segregating youth for ministering to their age-specific needs is both wise and effective, but integrating youth and seniors for friendship, fellowship, and service is equally wise and effective as well as mutually beneficial. Seniors ministry without sufficient intergenerational involvement deprives youth of what only seniors have to

156

offer them. Excessive age-segregation in ministry can also all too easily turn seniors ministry efforts into little more than an "old folks social club" that only propagates and perpetuates isolation and ageism while depriving seniors of life-giving inclusion.

It takes a supportive church leadership – There is a direct correlation between exceptional ministry with today's seniors and whether churches and church leaders publicly endorse as well as genuinely empower it. Without authentic support from the leadership, a seniors ministry program will, at best, only be treated more as an obligatory afterthought than an actual priority. Minimal vision, enthusiasm, endorsement, and budgetary support for seniors ministry will always and can only result in minimal effectiveness and results.

It takes someone's undivided attention – Ministry with today's seniors deserves and requires someone's full-time attention. All multi-staff churches should have someone on staff who works with seniors full-time or have this as a high priority goal. Imagine if churches pursued ministry with today's teens and children as lethargically as most pursue seniors ministry! Now imagine if churches began pursuing ministry with today's seniors with the same degree of vision and energy as is typically done with teens and children! Ministry with today's seniors, if it is to be exceptional, takes teamwork and cooperation. This is what it looks like. This is what it takes.

CONCLUSION

The people of God should be a people of God's *priorities*. Whatever is especially important to God should be especially important to us – regardless of how countercultural it may be or contrary to consensus within the local church. God's people should share in His priorities, because they long to be partakers in His divine nature. A core part of God's divine nature includes His extraordinary passion for seniors.

In a youth-focused culture, we have not given seniors the time, attention, or resources that they need or that God's high priority for seniors requires. Seniors are not only on God's short list of more important matters, but seniors are people, too! They have needs and struggle with faith. They need nurturing as well as encouragement. They have been gifted by God for service and need age-specific opportunities as well as empowerment for fully utilizing that giftedness. As a group, they need creative and innovative leadership for inspiring them to reach their potential.

The challenge before us, then, is to *begin* – to begin acknowledging the high priority status God has placed upon seniors and seniors ministry. If God is to be honored, we must begin recognizing the need for as well as the value, importance, and urgency of *exceptional* ministry with seniors. If His priorities are to be taken seriously, we must begin re-evaluating our church ministry budget and program priorities that so clearly slight seniors as revealed by the minimal amount of time, attention, and resources we devote to them. If we intend to make our best effort with seniors, we must begin envisioning a *new* paradigm perspective of seniors ministry - one that begins treating seniors and seniors ministry more like a priority than an afterthought. The challenge before us, then, is to begin developing and providing *exceptional* ministry with today's seniors ... because seniors are people, too.

47801498R00100

Made in the USA
Lexington, KY
12 August 2019